THE COLLINS WRITING PROGRAM

IMPROVING STUDENT PERFORMANCE

Through Writing and Thinking Across the Curriculum

John J. Collins, Ed.D.

W9-BBY-169

CEA Collins Education Associates West Newbury, Massachusetts

Copyright © 2007 by Collins Education Associates. All rights reserved.

The Collins Writing Program: Improving Student Performance Through Writing and Thinking Across the Curriculum is a revised and expanded version of *Developing Writing and Thinking Skills Across the Curriculum* originally published in 1992.

The purchase of this guide entitles the individual teacher to reproduce the parent letter and the assignments and focus sheets in Chapter Three and Chapter Four for classroom use, but does not permit reproduction in any part for an entire school, district or system, or for commercial use. With the exception of the assignments in Chapters Three and Four and the Focus Sheets that accompany them, no part of this publication may be reproduced or transmitted in any form or by any means, electronic or mechanical, including photocopy, recording, or information storage and retrieval system, without permission in writing from the author.

For information about the products, workshops, and consulting services available from Collins Education Associates LLC (CEA), call us at 1-800-932-4477, visit our website at www.collinsed.com, or contact us at 320 Main Street, P.O. Box 957, West Newbury, Massachusetts 01985.

ISBN: 978–0–9802312–0–5

2 3 4 5 6 7 8 9 0   ITP 17,500

10/08

Contents

Introduction

This book, *The Collins Writing Program,* is an expanded version of the highly successful *Developing Writing and Thinking Skills Across the Curriculum* (over 200,000 copies sold) originally published in 1992. Since the original publication, my colleagues and I have presented more than ten thousand workshops, conducted countless model lessons to demonstrate the program, and facilitated teacher discussions about writing skills in every imaginable school setting. As a result, we have learned a great deal about the strengths of this program and have been asked a lot of questions. This new book answers these questions and provides help to teachers, schools, or school systems that want to implement a coordinated writing across the curriculum program.

During the last twenty-five years, we have seen a shift from a demand for writing workshops primarily for ELA teachers to a demand for whole school or district workshops with teachers in every content area. The shift is driven by two separate factors: the expansion and change in the way we test students and the recognition that writing improves student learning. Anyone who has been teaching over the last few years has seen a dramatic expansion in the number of grades tested and in the very nature of the tests themselves. Tests now have open or constructed response questions where students must not only create an answer to the question but explain the answer or the process used to get the answer. With the addition of writing tests on the SAT and ACT, our only true national tests, writing has joined with reading as the second essential test-taking skill. If students cannot write, they cannot pass many state tests no matter how well they read or know the content.

But more important than the driving force of testing, writing has become a predominant focus because educators are recognizing that writing helps students understand and remember content like no other teaching technique. Douglas Reeves describes the powerful effects of writing on student achievements in his book *101 Questions & Answers About Standards, Assessments, and Accountability* where he describes his research of 90/90/90 schools. These are schools that are "quite unusual because their student populations include at least 90% free and reduced lunch students, 90% minority students, and 90% or more of students who meet or exceed state academic standards" (p. 121). He found that these schools shared four characteristics:

> They shared a *laser-like focus on student achievement*, an issue that
> dominated every faculty meeting, staff development presentation, and
> even the casual discussions among teachers and administrators. These
> schools *emphasized student writing*, with weekly writing assessments

and a common scoring guide, or rubric, to provide clear feedback on student performance. The teachers routinely *collaborated on scoring* so that they were able to give consistent feedback to the students. Students were afforded *multiple opportunities* to succeed on assignments.

Mike Schmoker writes passionately about the power of writing in *Results Now*, a book length critique of the state of literacy education in our country. He makes a plea for reading and writing to be at the center of the curriculum in all subjects. He states:

> The value of writing becomes clear only when we understand how it enables students to connect the dots in their knowledge. A deeper look at writing reveals its impact on our ability to learn and think at the highest levels, across the disciplines. Writing literally makes students smarter. We don't hear nearly enough about these benefits in education courses.... The very act of writing—and revising—teaches us to iden- tify and correct contradictions, to refine and improve and clarify our thoughts—*to think* (Hillocks, 1987). Writing may very well exercise the critical faculties in a way that can't be matched (pp. 62–63).

The problem is clear—we need to ask our students to write more. But to demand more writing and thinking, especially writing, requires more teacher work in an unending cycle of assignment giving, student response, and teacher feedback—sometimes for more than one hundred and fifty students. The time needed to complete just one cycle can be overwhelming. Yet if a teacher were to give assignments requiring written products without evaluating them, students, being only human, would stop completing the assignments or would do them in a perfunctory way. Academic tasks performed without adequate feedback can be counterproductive.

Schmoker provides a general answer:

> A drastic shift and a new awareness are needed here. As Anne-Marie Hall advises, "Write more; grade less" (1994). The research is strong that students are far better off when we score their work for only one or two criteria that we have just finished teaching carefully and explic- itly—and with the help of exemplars that add immensely to our best attempts to describe or define "voice" or "effective transitions" or "thoughtfully placed details" in a paragraph. Students need limited amounts of specific feedback—and they need it quickly, with the opportunity to correct or revise. Marzano and others have shown that we can be vastly more effective while spending only a fraction of the time we now spend on grading (pp. 168–169).

This book presents a model for a writing-across-the-curriculum/writing-to-learn program that explains exactly how to "write more—grade less" by defining five types of writing assignments and the outcomes expected for each. The Collins Writing Program has been designed for *real teachers* working under *real conditions*. My goal is to give teachers, schools, and districts a *unified, research-based program* that *can be used in all classrooms in all subject areas from grades four to twelve.** To achieve this goal, the program provides techniques that require the student to be the intellectual worker in the room. This is a challenging, demanding program for students—not for teachers.

The Collins Writing Program is not designed to turn all teachers into English teachers. Science, math, foreign language, career and technical education, health teachers, and others all have more than enough of their own content to cover. Rather, this program is designed to help teachers in all content areas help students achieve academically by requiring students to think on paper. Teachers accomplish this goal by using frequent, usually short, writing assignments to increase students' involvement in lessons, check on their understanding of concepts, or promote their thinking about content.

Here are some examples of writing assignments that the program suggests students might do to engage actively in the content of the lesson:

- List relevant information they "know" about a new concept or topic just before it is presented to them

- Put a concept from the text or another source into their own words—to "translate" it or summarize it

- Make a connection between a concept from class and something else they know about or have experienced in their own lives

- Explain how ideas are similar (despite their differences) or different (despite their similarities)

- Give an example that illustrates a general statement or give a general statement that explains some examples

In addition to having students write about the content of the course, the program can be used to encourage them to reflect on what they are doing to take respon-

---

* The Collins Writing Program is a K to 12 program, but I have found it impossible to write a specific, practical book for teachers that covers this wide range of grades. Therefore, the book you are reading is focused on grades 4 to 12. Gary Chadwell, my longtime associate, has adapted this book for grades K to 5 in *Developing an Effective Writing Program for the Elementary Grades.* It is available from Collins Education Associates. Our website, collinsed.com, provides information about all of our products and additional research and studies that support the effectiveness of our approach.

sibility for their own learning and understanding. Here are some examples of writing assignments that can help students become more reflective learners:

- Write about an assignment they've been given—what approach they might take or problems they think they might have

- Write about an upcoming test to find out what they don't fully understand and what they feel they do know

- Write about a test they just took, before the results are in, to reflect on their level of knowledge and understanding

- Write about their progress in class and their involvement in discussions and other activities—perhaps to make suggestions about how the class could be better for them and what they could do to make it that way

- Write about the personal significance of a subject—what they like best about it, how they'll use it someday

In addition to actively engaging students in the content of the course and requiring them to reflect on their approach to that content, the program can be used to refine listening and speaking skills. As you will see, some types of assignments require that the students read their writing out loud and listen critically to writing that is being read to them. These are extremely important steps, not only because they improve the quality of the final written product, but because they reinforce two skills—listening and speaking—that should be considered the most essential skills we teach, along with thinking and writing.

The Collins Writing Program has six chapters. "Chapter One: Five Types of Writing Assignments" provides a detailed description of the different types of writing assignments that form the basis of the program. "Chapter Two: Creating Types Three and Four Writing Assignments" explains how to create assignments that, because of the elements they contain, actually help to develop student writers. "Chapter Three: Essential Writing Assignments" describes four assignments that can become the bases of an effective writing program in any subject area. "Chapter Four: Highly Recommended Assignments" describes seven assignments that help teachers engage students in thinking about their thinking and help teachers learn about their students on a more personal level. "Chapter Five: Classroom Snapshots: Adapting the Collins Writing Program to Your Students" describes how the program might be implemented in different classes with students of different levels of experience, responsibility and motivation. Finally, "Chapter Six: Clarifying Expectations Outside the Classroom" discusses the need for clear communication about the program's expectations, especially to parents.

Five Types of Writing Assignments

This chapter describes the five different types of writing assignments that make up the Collins Writing Program. These assignments fall on a continuum from Type One to Type Five: Type One writing emphasizes idea generation without attention to the craft of writing, while Type Five emphasizes close attention to all aspects of craft and content. Each type has a different purpose; therefore, it is important for teachers to be certain about the type of writing they want and to communicate clearly to students which type is expected.

For years, researchers who studied learning processes have known that it is best to separate the creative (idea generating) and critical (idea evaluating) processes because the effective use of one hinders the effective use of the other. The system described in this chapter defines different types of writing and, by doing so, removes the psychological barriers to creativity by establishing times when it is all right to be "just creative" (Type One), times when a controlled progression of creative and critical thought are required (Types Two through Four), and times when the critical function is at its peak (Type Five).

The program helps students grow as thinkers and writers because it states explicitly what students must do to be successful. It takes away one of the primary obstacles to good writing: fear—fear of evaluation by unknown or hidden criteria and fear of failure. In addition to developing valuable thinking, learning, and writing skills, another major benefit of this program is that it saves teachers time. Writing assignments cease to be a punishment for teachers, who must prove to students that their work "counts" by correcting and evaluating every line. The Collins Writing Program provides a way for teachers to quickly evaluate student work and still have it count.

Type One Writing

DEFINITION: Type One writing is writing to get ideas on paper, brainstorming. It is the idea generating, recollecting, data gathering, exploring, or questioning phase of the writing and thinking process. Type One writing is timed and requires a minimum number of items or lines, a quota. Questions and/or guesses are permitted. Evaluated with a check (✔) or minus (—).

Type One writing is the perfect response to the question, how do we get students to write more without overwhelming the teacher? It's a way to make writing a natural occurrence. In her book, *The Nine Rights of Every Writer*, Vicki Spandel has the "right to write badly" as one of her nine rights. She goes on to say,

> In many classrooms, writing is an event: ***Time for writing!***
> The more we adopt this approach, the more unnatural we make
> writing feel—and the more pressure we put on students to make
> every writing act a performance to remember. . . . Our students
> will be stronger, better writers when it feels as natural to write in
> school as it feels to read, and when it is as integral to learning in
> all subjects (p. 71).

Of course a conscientious teacher may ask if frequent, ungraded writing makes any real difference in the quality of students' writing. Professional writers have long advocated free writing as a critical technique, and in a carefully designed study published in *Education and Treatment of Children*, Kasper-Ferguson and Moxley found that timed free writing periods dramatically improved the quality of student writing in the fourth grade. Their results showed "an examination of writing samples over time from students with the highest and lowest writing rates showed improved writing quality in terms of more concrete details and more sophisticated organization" (p. 249). It's powerful when conventional wisdom and carefully designed research studies complement one another.

Most Type One writing assignments are completed in class in less than ten minutes and are a great way to overcome writer's block. Typically they follow the rules of brainstorming by requiring students to write a specified amount in a specified time. Unlike brainstorming, Type One writing is usually done individually and many times without benefit of a class discussion. An important objective of Type One writing is to give everyone time to think about a topic. It can also quiet down highly verbal students (the 20 percent who do 80 percent of the talking) and provide teachers with a sense of how much students know about a particular area or topic.

Type One writing assignments commonly replace or precede classroom discussion. For example, one of the most effective uses of this type of writing is at the beginning of a unit. Rather than introducing the unit with a lecture or asking a class of students to tell what they know about the unit, a teacher asks all students to write a specified number of lines about everything they know about the topic. "If you do not know much or, for that matter, anything about the topic, write questions." I sometimes follow Type One assignments with an activity that asks a few individual students to read their papers while the class categorizes the ideas into three columns: facts about the topic, questions about the topic, and miscellaneous. While one student reads, the others listen and tell me where to list what was just read. Students must be active listeners to categorize and evaluate the ideas being read. It's a wonderful way to start any lesson, does not require at-home preparation, and gets students talking, listening, and thinking about a topic they will be studying.

Format for Type One Writing: Type One writing requires just one draft. Students only need to put their names on the first line, right-hand side, and "Type One" on the first line, left-hand side of their papers, and remember to skip lines. Masters with the correct format for the different types of writing are at the back of this book. You may find it helpful to copy some of these pages until the students have the proper format mastered.

Form: Type One writing can take almost any form, but it is often a list, rambling essay, or personal reflection. Some teachers call it a learning log or response journal, but because of the quota and time limit, it tends to be more structured than the traditional log or journal. Type One writing can even take the form of a graphic organizer or chart where students display information in a graphic form. It can mix facts and questions. While the most obvious Type One assignments respond to directions like, "Tell me everything you know about a particular topic, or predict what will happen if . . . ," a more interesting use of Type One writing asks students to write in an imaginative/narrative style—writing to tell a story—rather than in an analytical/expository style— writing to explain or prove to a teacher that the student knows something. For example, a social studies teacher might ask students to write fifteen to twenty lines of dialogue between two historical figures who have met in the afterlife and are sharing thoughts and experiences. The important thing to remember is that these pieces do not have to be polished—they just have to be attempted.

Audience: The only audience for Type One writing is the student writer. The teacher plays the role of a quick evaluator who does not carefully read the paper but checks to see if the amount of writing required was generated and that the student attempted to interact with the topic. Teachers typically will skim a sample of Type Ones from a class to get a sense of the class' prior knowledge in relationship to a new unit.

Evaluation: The only evaluation criterion for Type One writing is that each student must write something in an atmosphere of either no risk or relatively no risk. For students who are not very fluent writers or who need a concrete goal, the sole criterion is the number of written lines, written within a time limit. It is important to use number of written lines rather than sentences. A teacher who requires sentences must read and correct sentence structure, and that is not the purpose of Type One writing. For example, the teacher gives the assignment, "Write ten lines telling what you know about Siberia, and if you cannot think of ten lines of information, list questions." Then the teacher can evaluate the assignment by simply looking at the length and need not read it to see if it was written in sentences. The objective is to help students discover what they know, not to see if their writing is in complete sentences.

Example A, on page 6, is a Type One response written by an eighth grade student to the assignment about Siberia. It has been evaluated with a check because it has ten written lines. Obviously, it was easy to evaluate and the student made it easier by numbering the lines. The correctness of the content and the level of writing skills are not at issue here. The student simply was required to think about a topic and capture questions and possible areas of knowledge or misunderstanding. By using this Type One assignment, the teacher had a chance to assess what the student knew at the time. If the student had not written ten lines, the grade would be a minus. Evaluation for Type One writing should be kept very simple, based on one easily observable trait. An extensive list of possible Type One assignments is on pages 7 to 9. You may want to keep a copy of these pages at your desk for ready reference.

FAQ

Type One writing has a time limit. I have special needs students who are not to have timed tests. What do you suggest?

ANSWER: Because Type One assignments are supposed to be non-threatening (no right or wrong answers) and are graded simply, I would try to modify the time restriction for Type One assignments. My guess is that the non-timed requirement is for tests and quizzes and Type One can easily be considered an exception. But if everything must be non-timed, I have had good success changing the quota (ten lines in four minutes) so that a student in question does not need to produce as much (say, five lines) within the time limit. In this way you have made a reasonable accommodation and have given the student an opportunity to practice writing under time-pressure—a life-long skill. The value of the time limit is that it helps students get down to work immediately and discourages perfectionism because of the pressure of the time limit. I think of Type One as an effort grade rather than an academic grade. ■

How important is the correct formatting of the papers?

ANSWER: The format is a means to an end, not the end. The Collins Writing Program is not about how to head a paper, but if students learn to head the paper the same way, it has significant advantages. First, the heading becomes one less thing to worry about. No student energy needs to be expended trying to figure out what the teacher wants, and when it becomes automatic, there are fewer papers without names; by the second year of the program, it's routine. When students get to Type Three and Type Four writing, the papers have the student record focus correction areas (explanation to follow). If the students write the focus correction areas, the teacher has proof the students know the evaluative criteria and the points. Also, parents and other interested individuals (other teachers, school administrators, curriculum coordinators, etc.) know about your standards for a particular paper. The heading of the paper communicates, at a glance, the type of writing and the evaluation standards.

In addition to the heading, we get questions about the necessity of skipping lines. I am a proponent of skipping lines for a number of reasons: first, skipping lines provides space for students to edit without making a mess of their papers. I find many students are unable to deal with an extensively edited draft because it becomes so messy. They toss the draft away and begin with a fresh sheet. Skipping lines permits editing that is easier to understand, recopy, or retype. Because Type One writing is likely to generate information that could become the basis of Type Two through Type Five writing assignments, having space for revisions, corrections, and elaboration is critical. A second reason to have students skip lines is that papers are easier to read. It has been my experience that double-spaced papers take approximately twenty percent less time to read than single-spaced papers. Any formatting system that can save twenty percent of a teacher's time is worth instituting. A third reason is that double spacing allows more room for teacher or peer comments, and the comments can be placed so that they are easier to understand. Finally, if papers are double-spaced they can be used later for editing practice on new skills. If students keep papers in folders, they have a great source of relevant practice sheets. ▪

Tip!

My favorite follow-up to a Type One writing assignment is the below-the-line activity. In this activity, the students draw a line across the paper where the Type One writing has ended. They then partner up with another student and share each other's writing, adding a specified number of additional written lines "below the line," thus adding to their original list. I find that asking students to "add three additional lines of information or questions that you did not have on your original list" focuses the discussions and makes the students more accountable than just asking students to share.

EXAMPLE A

Type One   ✓   Joe Smith

10/15

X 1	Siberia is one of 11 states that used to make the
X 2	up the Soviet Union. It is a cold poor country
X 3	that has a few oil sourses. What are some
X 4	political leaders? What are the people like?
X 5	What do they eat? (fish?) What is their
X 6	financial status? What is their currency.
X 7	What are activities kids do to pass the time?
X 8	What is their schooling like? What are some
X 9	problems that face the region? What are
X 10	current things happening. What are some
X 11	cities? What famous people are from Siberia?
X 12	Would they rather live in the US? Why?

Sample Type One Writing Questions

Type One writing gets ideas on paper—brainstorming. Type One is **timed** and requires a **minimum number** of items or lines. Questions and/or guesses are permitted. Evaluated with a check (✔) or minus (—).

For Activating Prior Knowledge:

▶ In eight* lines or more (or five or ten lines, depending on the time you want to take), write the things you know or questions you have about _____.

▶ Even though we have not read or discussed it yet, what does the term (or concept or phrase) _____ mean to you? Fill at least four* lines.

▶ What do you think this (picture, formula, abbreviation, notation, chart, word, mark, or phrase) means? Why do you think so? Fill seven* lines or more.

▶ What do you think a _____ looks like? Describe it in six* lines or more.

▶ How do you think a _____ behaves (or is solved or is constructed)? Fill eight* lines or more.

For Reflecting About Learning:

▶ What were the most important (or interesting, surprising) points to you from yesterday's discussion about _____? Fill six* lines or more.

▶ On the topic we discussed yesterday, fill eight* lines or more about the ideas you understood best. Least.

▶ Think about and write down two* "hard questions" about _____.

▶ On last night's homework, explain what was the hardest part for you to solve (or understand, complete, read, collect, and so on)? Fill five* lines or more.

▶ If you were going to solve (or do or read or study) _____, what would you do differently? Give your explanation in at least six* lines.

---

*To enhance the brainstorming aspects of this Type One prompt, establish a quota of writing and time limit appropriate for the task.

▶ Now that we have finished our unit on _____, make a list of at least ten* terms that would appear in a book chapter on this topic.

▶ What went well with your group project (or experiment or performance)? What would improve the group's work? Fill five* lines or more.

▶ What kinds of questions (or problems, reading assignments, laboratory activities, new vocabulary, writing assignments, and so on) are hard for you? Fill six* lines or more.

▶ As you think about what we did in class (or lab) today, what was (the easiest, most fun, most challenging, something you would like to do again, differently)? Fill at least seven* lines.

▶ Based on today's discussion, do a 3-2-1 reflection. Write down three things you found interesting, two things that were a bit confusing, and one thing you would like to know more about.

▶ What are two* ways you would go about solving this problem?

▶ Write at least four* examples of _____.

▶ What are three* ways we can get the same (result, solution, answer, outcome)?

▶ List three* (tools, formulas, instruments, reference materials) you think were used to accomplish this.

▶ When you are preparing for a test, what techniques do you use to help you remember important facts? Fill six* lines or more.

▶ Think about the test you just completed and how you prepared for it. What should you have spent more time studying? Less time? Why? Fill six* lines or more.

▶ What are some of the things you do that make you a good (reader, writer, test taker, problem solver, study mate)? Fill five* lines or more.

▶ Describe something that you can do better now than you could last year. Fill six* lines or more.

▶ When I teach this unit on _____ to next year's class, what do you think I could do to make it better? Tell me in ten* lines or more.

_____

*To enhance the brainstorming aspects of this Type One prompt, establish a quota of writing and time limit appropriate for the task.

For Predicting:

▶ For the upcoming test, what questions do you think I might ask that would require a short, written answer (as opposed to a multiple-choice, true-false, or matching answer)? Give at least four* questions.

▶ In five* lines, predict what would happen if _____. Explain why you think so.

▶ In five* lines, describe what might have caused the scene you see in this picture.

▶ Before we (go on this field trip, conduct this experiment, study this unit, collect this data), write eight* lines about some of the things you hope to find out.

For Making Connections:

▶ What relationship does _____ have with current events or your daily life at home or school? Fill at least six* lines.

▶ How do you think _____ and _____ are related? Fill five* lines or more.

▶ How is _____ (this type of problem, concept) similar to _____ (another type of problem, concept)? Fill seven* lines or more.

For Creative Thinking:

▶ What do you think someone in this situation (in a story, news event, and so on) would be thinking? Be worried about? Be happy about? What do you think the other person in this situation would be thinking? Fill at least eight* lines.

▶ Describe a way of doing this routine task (such as reviewing home-work, passing out lab materials, distributing calculators, signing out instruments or supplies) so that it would be more interesting or efficient to do. Tell me in six* lines or more.

▶ What if (electricity emitted sound waves, numbers 0-10 had assigned colors, copy machines did not exist, houses could not be built with right angles, and so on)? What would life be like? Fill at least ten* lines.

___

*To enhance the brainstorming aspects of this Type One prompt, establish a quota of writing and time limit appropriate for the task.

Type Two Writing

DEFINITION: Type Two writing shows that the writer knows something about a topic or has thought about the topic; it is best used as a quiz. It usually has a number in the question.

Type Two writing assignments ask for definitions, facts, explanations, opinions supported with details, evaluative comments, or new applications. It is identical to the open response or constructed response questions on many state tests. In Type Two writing the evaluation criterion is that the content must be clear and correct. Because no points are deducted for spelling, punctuation, and capitalization, Type Two writing is an ideal mode for some students who have weak mechanical skills. In reality, there is a natural limit to the number of writing mistakes a student can make on Type Two writing because the response might be unintelligible. Good ideas will be lost if the writing is terribly poor. But Type Two writing asks teachers to "separate the dancer from the dance" and evaluate the content, not the way the content is expressed.

Type Two writing is best used in lieu of individual questions to students in class to encourage active participation by all students in the same way Type One writing does. For example, rather than ask a few students if they know the answer to a question, give a Type Two assignment that asks all students to answer a question in writing. You then have a choice of evaluation strategies depending upon the importance of the questions and the amount of time available. (The section on evaluation that follows provides some options.)

The key to successful Type Two writing assignments is that the prompt or question must be clear and have a definite answer. This does not mean that the answer must be a verbatim response from the text or class notes. Rather, the best Type Two assignments help students make their own meaning by translating concepts into their own words. Vague questions encourage vague answers, and vague answers are difficult and time consuming to evaluate. Below are some examples of Type Two assignments in different subject areas.

- From our class discussion, give a one- or two- sentence definition of sportsmanship. Then describe a situation from your own experience that illustrates your definition.

- Give a five- to ten-line summary of last night's reading. Include two to three main ideas.

- List at least ten materials you will need to conduct this experiment.

- Explain at least four steps you would take to solve the problem on the board and then use the steps to solve it.

- Explain two mistakes that a student made when creating this graph.

Format for Type Two Writing: As in Type One writing, students only need to put their names on the first line, right-hand side, and "Type Two" on the first line, left-hand side of their papers. Remember to skip lines to leave space to refine the answer and make it easier to read. There is only one draft.

Form: Because Type Two writing is primarily used to quiz students, it most frequently takes the form of an open response question, list, or definition. Type Two assignments should encourage students to write what they know or how they feel in response to a prompt, but discourage them from adding lines or pages to pad their answers. Good answers or ideas can be obscured in the fog of their own words. As students have experience with Type Two writing, they will begin to learn the distinction between padding a response and using writing as a tool to develop and elaborate ideas.

Audience: The audience for Type Two writing is the teacher, who has high expectations about the content of the writing but not about how flawlessly the content is expressed.

Evaluation: Type Two writing is best for a question that requires a limited, specific, predictable response. Open-ended questions are served better with Type One writing, where the writer has free rein, or with Type Three writing, where the writer knows the specific criteria for success. *I have found that questions or prompts that have quantity specification are good candidates for Type Two writing.* For example, list the *three* possible causes for this chemical reaction, define *three* of the five terms on the board, explain the *two* main points we discussed during yesterday's class, or indentify *two* errors in this solution.

Evaluation systems for Type Two writing should be kept as simple as possible, permitting the teacher to skim the paper looking for the correct response. I find that the best evaluation systems are point systems because they are quick and easy to use. The teacher and the situation will determine how difficult the point system should be, but for many students who would rather sit back and relax, especially during last period, a Type Two writing assignment can be a real wake-up call. Of course, there are a number of alternative evaluation strategies for Type Two writing (e.g., points for each correct answer, letter grade off for each definition missed), but to be successful they should be simple, quick, and require that the teacher only skim the written work looking for the "correct" response.

Type Two writing is quiz writing and should not be used for a major test. The more frequently Type Two writing is given, the better. Students get used to the approach and the teacher can get enough Type Two writing grades from each student during the course of a marking period to be able to use these results to make a report card grade as reliable as possible. Type Two grades are also very helpful in determining the effort grade.

As the frequency of Type Two writing increases, the number of papers that the teacher needs to evaluate decreases. For example, if a teacher decides that evaluating five Type Two responses per student per quarter is reasonable, then that teacher can give twenty Type Two writing assignments and collect only a twenty-five percent sample each time. Yet, the students will have to engage in twenty writing and thinking experiences, giving each one maximum effort because they will never know if an individual piece will be collected.

It is the potential for frequent, easy-to-evaluate writing assignments that gives Type Two writing its real power. In the April 1991 issue of *Educational Leadership*, Frank Dempster's "Synthesis of Research on Reviews and Tests" examines all the research available on the effects of testing on student understanding and retention of content. He states: "Research on learning—specifically research on the effectiveness of tests—has found consistently that tests do more than test; they also promote learning."

He goes on to provide details about his findings: 1) testing, especially if it is conducted soon after material is introduced, promotes learning; 2) frequent, spaced testing results in higher levels of achievement than does infrequent testing; and 3) the use of cumulative questions on tests is one of the keys to effective learning. He concludes his review by stating, "More frequent use of properly spaced reviews and tests in the classroom can dramatically improve classroom learning and retention. Another potential benefit . . . suggests that spaced repetitions encourage highly constructive thinking." Dempster's conclusions should not be news to teachers for whom the question has always been how to create and evaluate frequent tests, especially if they are essay tests.

Tip! One simple way to begin implementation of the Collins Writing Program is to ask students to write down two questions that could be fairly asked at the beginning of tomorrow's class. Creating two questions is a Type One assignment because there is no one correct answer. In fact, I am frequently surprised by what my students think is important in class versus what I am attempting to teach.

These Type Ones are great closure activities. Don't be surprised if students ask if they can use their notes to create the questions. And, of course, you should let them—it's a great review. At the end of class, walk around to make sure that students wrote the required number of questions, giving a check or a minus and call on a few students to read what they wrote. When you hear some good questions, point them out, write them in your plan book and ask them the next day as a Type Two quiz. When I gave the Type Two quiz the next day, I usually rolled a die to see what row or group's paper I would collect and grade so that I did not have to grade everyone's papers. No one knows whose quiz will be collected, it's always random, and I can usually grade four to six Type Twos between classes. This technique of creating questions at the end of class and asking one at the beginning of the next encourages note taking, daily review of notes, ongoing formative assessment, and a check to see if the class was clear—a terrific payoff!

More recent research compiled by David Glenn in the June 8, 2007 *Chronicle of Higher Education* confirms and deepens Dempster's conclusions. In "You Will Be Tested On This," Glenn summarized the effects of "effortful retrieval":

> A student who has just read a complex article full of unfamiliar facts about 17th-century Poland will retain that information much better if he is quizzed—thus forcing him to retrieve the data from memory—than if he simply rereads the article two or three times. . . . Instructors should take a few minutes to give quizzes, preferably in short-answer format, at the beginning or end of each class session. . . . Instructors might consider it a nuisance to construct and grade the quizzes, he says, but it's far worse to allow students to go 12 weeks between hearing a lecture and coughing up facts on a final exam. Students who wait to cram for a final exam rarely retain the material over the long term, even if they perform reasonably well on the final (p. A14).

Example B is a Type Two response written by an eighth grade student in response to the question, "In a short composition, write what you know about Siberia, including and numbering ten facts." The evaluation of the paper was 60 because the student only listed six facts. "Siberia is the most exciting place in the world" is, of course, an opinion, not a fact.

EXAMPLE B

Type Two   (60)   Joe Smith
                                                                                10/19

X
1   Although it is the largest region in the Soviet
X
2   Union It only has 9% of the population. The
X
3/4 Population is 25 million Lung cancer is a big
X
5   problem in Siberia Siberia is about the same
X
6   size as the U.S.A. Siberia is the most
X
7   exciting place in the world. Siberia is very

     desolate.

The evaluation was based solely on whether or not there are ten correctly stated facts about Siberia in the piece and not about the missed periods. This type of assignment is better than a typical multiple choice exercise because it requires students to assemble the information themselves and can be given spontaneously without the need to prepare a multiple choice test. Also, it is very easy to grade because, in this case, the criteria are limited to ten facts and the student has numbered the facts, or at least what he thought were the facts, about Siberia.

A helpful list of Type Two prompts is on pages 15 to 16. The questions have been arranged to reflect the six categories of Bloom's Taxonomy. As you can see, Type Two questions do not need to be limited to the lower levels of Bloom's Taxonomy (remembering and understanding) but can also be used at the higher levels (evaluating and creating). You may want to keep a copy of these pages at your desk for ready reference.

Sample Type Two Writing Questions

Type Two writing shows that the writer knows something about a topic or has thought about the topic. It is the correct answer to a specific question, graded as a quiz. **One draft.**

Note: Type Two writing prompts can span the full range of Bloom's Taxonomy of Educational Objectives, from remembering to creating. (The taxonomy was revised in the 1990's by Lorin Anderson, a student of Bloom's. The categories here reflect the revised taxonomy.)

Remembering—recalling information:

▶ Define five* _____ key words.

▶ List five* facts about_____.

▶ Describe three* characteristics of all _____.

▶ Describe two* ways that _____ occurs in everyday living.

▶ Locate three* (cities, rivers, attributes, etc.) of _____.

Understanding—explaining ideas or concepts:

▶ Paraphrase (write in your own words using about the same number of words) the following passage. Be sure to include the two* key points.

▶ Summarize the three* most important points from our class yesterday (or today's class or last night's reading).

▶ In your own words, write the meaning of _____ in a way that a classmate would understand and be able to answer on a test.

▶ Explain the three* steps that must be taken in order to get an answer to this problem (or question, situation, etc.).

Applying—using information in another familiar situation:

▶ What two* strategies that we have talked about might you use to (solve, connect, figure out, repair, set, etc.) the following?

▶ Describe at least two materials* (or resources, chemicals, colors, instruments, tools, sources, etc.) needed to do (or solve) the problem.

Analyzing—breaking information into parts to explore relationships:

▶ Explain two* ways that _____ and _____ are similar.

▶ Describe three* ways that _____ and _____ are different.

_____

*or some other appropriate number

▶ _____ and _____ are alike in some ways and different in others. Describe two* ways they are similar and two ways* they are different.

▶ Explain two* ways that you could tell the difference between a _____ and a _____.

▶ Tell three* things wrong with this statement (or work order, blue-print, description, problem solution, lab report, etc.).

▶ Explain two* ways that data could be shown to support this answer.

▶ Describe a pitfall to avoid in doing this experiment (or problem, design, performance, lab report, etc.).

Evaluating—justifying a decision, checking, critiquing, judging:

▶ Explain two* reasons why I would not give this answer full credit on a test.

▶ Give two* reasons why this cannot be a correct answer for this problem (or question). Explain.

▶ Give three* reasons you can tell this is not a _____.

▶ What are three* things you could change to make this sketch (or comparison, blueprint, proof, explanation, pattern, recipe, report, etc.) better?

▶ Tell three* reasons why _____ can't or doesn't work. Explain.

▶ Rank and justify our ranking of these three* projects.

Creating—generating new ideas, products, or ways of viewing things:

▶ All but one of the following operations (or animals, objects, events, tools, ingredients, etc.) belongs to a category because they have several common characteristics. Give this category a name and give two* reasons why one does not belong in this category.

▶ If the answer is _____, write two* questions that would go with that answer.

▶ What two* changes would you recommend in yesterday's class that would help make the material more clear (interesting, relevant to your lives, etc.)?

▶ What are three* possible results if Hitler had won the war?

_____
*or some other appropriate number.

Type Three Writing

DEFINITION: Type Three writing is writing that has substantive content and meets up to three specific standards called focus correction areas. Writers of Type Three assignments must create a draft, read it out loud, and review it to see if the draft meets the following criteria: completes the assignment, is easy to read, and avoids problems in the focus correction areas. Revising and editing are done on the draft.

Type Three writing is the most versatile of all the types because it is efficient to assign, defines the standards that students need to meet to be successful, and is easy to evaluate and grade. Type Three writing assignments (as well as Type Four, as we see in the next section) move students from merely producing and recording ideas to refining the way they present ideas. When students finish a first draft of a Type Two writing assignment, they are done. When they finish the first draft of a Type Three assignment, the real work is just beginning.

Helping students refine their written work requires two steps that differentiate Type Three writing from Type Two: focus correcting and oral reading/editing. Each of these two will be discussed in some detail in the following paragraphs, but first I would like to place them in the process. When students have completed a draft of a Type Three assignment, they must read it out loud to themselves and ask themselves three key questions that require them to determine if they (1) completed the assignment given, (2) produced a readable work, and (3) met the assigned criteria.

In essence, Type Three writing assignments provide a structured editing process for drafts. Because oral reading and focus correcting make up the core of the Collins Writing Program, the following section will elaborate on them in detail.

▶ Oral Reading/Editing

Reading their own work out loud is the single most effective way to help students revise and edit. As Peter Elbow, a well-published and nationally recognized authority on writing instruction states in the January 1992 issue of *Writing Teacher*, "When [students] read their words out loud, they can feel when a sentence works well or badly—through the feeling in their mouth and the sound in their ear. Most writers agree that the mouth and the ear are the main organs through which students learn to write better" (p. 72).

After students complete a first draft of a Type Three assignment, they read it out loud to themselves, listening for three things:

● Did I complete the assignment?
● Does the composition sound right? Is it easy to read?
● Do I have problems with the focus correction areas?

The first two questions get to the basic issues of content and flow. The third helps direct students to the focus correction areas, which must be clear to them before they begin their first drafts (see discussion that follows). Based on their answers to these questions, they make revisions on their drafts (which have been double-spaced to allow room for edits). For some, oral reading may seem like such an obvious step that it appears self-evident or simplistic. "Of course, students will read their work before they hand it in." But, sadly, many don't! Oral reading needs to be institutionalized classroom-by-classroom until it becomes a routine part of all students' behavior.

The teacher should model the reading of papers out loud for students, reading slowly and carefully, listening to the words and placing a check mark in the margin to indicate rough spots that need more revision. Teachers also need to listen to students as they practice reading out loud, making sure that students are reading slowly and accurately. It is possible to do oral reading in class with all students reading at once by having students read in a "one-foot voice," a voice that cannot be heard by someone more than one foot away. If each student reads in a one-foot voice, the noise level in the room will not be disruptive. Depending on the age of the students, it will take them from one to several opportunities to become comfortable with reading their work out loud.

Oral reading is critical for a successful Type Three writing experience. Donald Murray, considered by many the father of modern writing instruction and himself a prize-winning writer, discussed his writing practices in the April 1999 issue of the *English Journal*:

> I need to read aloud and write aloud. Voice, after meaning, is the
> most important element in effective writing. An individual human
> voice is what we seek in a text, that voice is what keeps us reading and
> makes us believe what is written. And I must help my student hear the
> shadow of the voice in the early drafts and remind my student to keep
> writing out loud so the heard quality of writing will rise from the page
> (p. 93).

Tip! Ask students to read their drafts from beginning to end without stopping to fix anything. "Stopping to fix" is the enemy of this strategy because it interrupts the flow of the reading. Writers who stop to fix or change as they read are much less likely to notice repetitions, omissions, or "doesn't sound right" passages. I ask students to simply put a checkmark in their paper if they see or hear something that they think needs attention. Then after they finish reading the entire composition, they can go back and address their concerns. To ensure that students take this process seriously, I suggest a quota of checkmarks. "Everyone should make at least ____ checkmarks."

In *Writing on Demand*, Ruggels and her colleagues expand on Murray's point by discussing the role of oral reading in revision.

> When we read the text over, we find ourselves mentally filling in explanations that aren't actually included in the writing. We imagine transitions where none exist, and unless we read aloud, it's easy to skip over clunky phrasing. These things happen because we read with our brains, not our eyes, and brains fill in what should be on the page and ignore the things that shouldn't be there (p. 101).

They go on to discuss oral reading in testing situations by making the following recommendations:

> Read your work aloud. This will slow you down enough to catch errors that would be difficult to see during silent reading. In a test environment, simply whisper to yourself. Since you won't have time to recopy your work, this is a quick way to make sure you eliminate glaring problems (p. 104).

Type Three writing is about hearing our voices rise from the page and applying the criteria of the focus correction areas.

▶ Focus Correcting*

Focus correcting is a selective approach to correcting student writing. With focus correcting, the teacher selects one, two, or three critical problem areas to focus on. Focus correcting concentrates both student and teacher attention on a few particular writing or thinking skills in any assignment. Ideally, teachers assign a particular focus correction area (FCA) often enough for students to become proficient users of the skill reflected in that FCA. The focus correction areas will change over time as students add to and refine their skills. Almost any aspect of writing/thinking can be selected as a focus correction area, from using details to support a thesis to writing a good summary statement to correct capitalization and punctuation.

When first introduced to the idea of focus correcting, many teachers are uncomfortable. Focus correcting runs contrary to our experience both as teachers and students, because correcting compositions has meant noting every error on every line. But think about the reality of the classroom. How often have you seen students examining a corrected paper, carefully looking for each error? Most students want to know the grade and be done with it. Focus correcting changes

---

* For additional information on focus correction areas, with research, examples, and information about essential FCA's, see my book *Selecting and Teaching Focus Correction Areas*, available from Collins Education Associates.

this attitude by helping students consider the quality of the paper with respect to a few clearly specified criteria, rather than an infinite number of highly subjective criteria.

Nevertheless, teachers also feel that by letting errors go, they are condoning mistakes or denying students the opportunity to learn. "If I don't tell them, how will they know it is wrong? We are adding to the decline of literacy!" Well, not necessarily. In *Engaging Ideas: The Professor's Guide to Integrating Writing, Critical Thinking, and Active Learning in the Classroom*, John Bean states:

> It might be comforting to know that teachers have a long tradition of complaining about errors in their students' writing and that the frequency of error has not risen appreciably. Connors and Lunsford (1988) have compared the types and frequency of errors of today's students with earlier studies from 1917 and 1930. Basing their study of today's students on a random sample of three thousand student essays collected nationwide in 1986, they found surprising consistency in the frequency of error across time. The error frequency rate in 1917 was 2.11 errors per hundred words; in 1930, it was 2.24 errors per hundred words; and in 1986, it was 2.26 errors per hundred words. Their conclusion: "College students are not making more formal errors in writing than they used to." (406) . . . The most significant difference discovered by Connors and Lunsford is that today's students make substantially more errors in spelling and in confusing of homonyms (to, two, too; it's, its), a phenomenon they attribute to declining familiarity with the visual look of the written page" (p. 406). Thus, the poor spelling of today's students, according to this hypothesis, reflects a decline in the amount of time spent reading (p. 60).

Furthermore, even when we take the time to mark all the errors, we rarely actually mark "all the errors." Few of us are trained as professional copy editors. We mark errors idiosyncratically. Again, Bean finds:

> Moreover, readers vary widely in the kinds of errors that bother them. Some teachers mark every instance of an apostrophe error but do not notice comma splices; others rail at fragments but apparently do not notice dangling modifiers. Some teachers get livid over "Everyone in the room raised their hands," while others prefer this form over the sexist "his hand" or the unwieldy "his or her hand" (p. 61).

Of course there are the few who have what Lynne Truss calls, in her surprise best-seller on punctuation *Eats, Shoots & Leaves*, the seventh sense. "We are like the little boy in the *Sixth Sense* who can see dead people, except that we can see dead punctuation" (p. 3). If you are feeling despair, it might help to quote Bean again, this time about what may be a surprising cause of error in student writing.

> A particularly illuminating discovery of composition research is the extent to which students' apparent skill level varies according to the cognitive complexity of the writing task. Schwalm (1985) has noted the relationship between error production and the difficulty level of a communication task in the examinations used by government language schools to categorize students' skill levels. An examinee might seem totally fluent in foreign language when making small talk; however, grammatical competence begins to drop off as the tasks become more complex and decreases dramatically when the examinee is asked to advance arguments, hypothesize, or handle abstractions. The more cognitively difficult the task, the more an examinee's sentence structure breaks down (p. 63).

Students do indeed have control over most conventions, but when they are given a task that involves cognitive complexity, their skills break down. Every coach knows that kids can do it in practice, but during the real game things fall apart. Likewise, with a new poetic form, research paper, or persuasive essay—skills vanish in the tumult of the complex task. But there is hope. Bean, once again:

> This phenomenon suggests that the early error-laden draft is a necessary step toward the writer's eventual mastery of the ideas and that once the ideas have become clearer, the sentence structure begins to clear up also (p.64).

In the Collins Writing Program, an early draft may be a Type Three assignment that gets its value from the effort students put in to try to explain their thinking. At that point, we can be happy with what we have and move on to new areas of the curriculum.

▶ Selecting Focus Correction Areas

Countless ways exist to organize writing skills, but using the four categories (content, organization, conventions, and style) shown here is a simple and effective way to get the job done.

The **content** category is the *what* of the writing. Content includes the quality of the information or ideas and the details used to support them. Content in technical or practical writing is usually easy to judge; content in fiction is more subjective. It is usually the content (reasons) of persuasive writing that persuades, and the content (plot) of a mystery story that entertains.

The **organization** category is the *order* of the writing. Organization includes what some teachers call unity, coherence, and emphasis or what others call logical order or sequence. In well-organized writing, the major points or ideas stand out, and the reader knows where he or she is going. A good test of well-organized writing is that it is easy to summarize.

The **convention** category has to do with the *appearance* of the writing. Conventions cover everything from legibility to spelling, from neatness to usage. Conventions have to do with the etiquette of writing, the respect for past practice. We don't wear brown shoes with a tuxedo and we don't write essays in pencil. Students can have the best organization and content in the world, but conventions can kill them.

The **style** category is the *personality* of the writing. It is the hardest aspect to define. It is everything that is left over after we have looked at content, organization, and conventions. Style is made up of word choice, sentence structure, variety, voice, and a lot more. Teachers must help students learn that they can go back to a piece of writing and change the way it looks, change the impression it makes on the reader, change even the texture and the feel of the writing. They can make it formal or informal, showy or plain, funny or serious.

The writer who wants to pay attention to style must ask himself or herself several important questions. Who is my reader or audience? What is my purpose in writing this piece? What impression do I want to make? The teacher frames these questions differently depending upon the age and writing ability of his or her students. Very young writers may be taught to follow what may be called the golden rule of writing: "Write for others the way you want to be written to." Older, more sophisticated students must be coached to move to the other side of the communication exchange: "Put yourself in the place of

Tip! The use of focus correction areas will help make evaluating papers more efficient, but reviewing one hundred plus papers is a time consuming and tedious process no matter how clearly the FCAs are stated; therefore, I have developed a technique to help me speed up the assessment of papers by telling students to indicate the FCAs I will be looking for by circling (especially helpful to find specific words, e.g., vocabulary or vivid verbs, etc.), underlining (great for thesis statements, metaphors, varied sentence beginnings, etc.), and brackets (for longer sections like interesting beginnings, strong conclusions, proofs in math, etc.). I also ask students to number the items on the margin so that I do not have to count. I find this practice not only helps me get through the papers more quickly, but it makes me more accurate by directing me to the FCA. It also requires the student to show me that they know what they have done.

Of course it is hard to get students of any age to remember to circle, underline, bracket, and number the FCAs, so I try to make an announcement right before I collect the papers to remind them to check to see if the annotations are complete. Over the years, these student annotations have saved me countless hours.

the reader." The more insightful the writer and reader, the more complex these style decisions become.

Listed here are sample focus correction areas related to content, organization, conventions, and style. Considering the grade level and your diagnosis of your students' writing skills, star a few FCAs that seem most critical to you. If a list does not mention the skills that your students need or if the skills are stated too generally, add skills or make them more specific.

▶ Sample Focus Correction Areas Related to Content

● Sufficient, relevant detail

● Technical vocabulary used and spelled correctly

● References current and reflect major resources

● _____

● _____

Note: The most obvious and critical FCA for content/thinking skills is, "Does the composition respond to the assignment?" This is so central to good writing that it is built into Type Three and Type Four assignments as the first question the writer asks after reading the paper out loud: "Did I complete the assignment?"

▶ Sample Focus Correction Areas Related to Organization

● Beginning and ending that establish focus and purpose

● Clear sequence of detail or information

● Paragraphing appropriate to the purpose

● Step-by-step organization (especially in practical, informative, or technical writing)

● Transitions for clarity

● Spatial order

● Clearly stated thesis

● Ideas developed in proportion to their importance

● Conclusion that reinforces, summarizes, or challenges

● _____

● _____

▶ Sample Focus Correction Areas Related to Conventions

● Complete sentences

● Standard usage

● Correct capitalization

● Legible penmanship

● Draft in correct form

● Proper use of internal punctuation

● _____

● _____

▶ Sample Focus Correction Areas Related to Style

● Sentence variety (Sentences too long? Confusing? Too short? Monotonous? Balance between long and short sentences? Balance between simple and complex? Do all the sentences begin the same way?)

● No unnecessary words

● Beginning that captures interest

● Avoidance of clichés

● Figurative language

● Powerful verbs

● Shows involvement of the writer

● _____

● _____

Note: "Is the paper easy to read out loud?" is the most critical style FCA. Because of the importance of reading out loud, it is built into Type Three and Type Four assignments as the first step after the first draft is complete. The writer must read his or her work out loud and ask, "Does the composition sound right? Is it easy to read?" James Kilpatrick states in *The Writer's Art*, "I have a theory about writing. It goes to the effect: The chief difference between good writing and better writing may be measured by the number of imperceptible hesitations the reader experiences as he goes along" (p. 29). Kilpatrick is correct. If a work can be read out loud without causing the reader to hesitate or stop completely, then stylistically it is usually quite good.

When creating FCAs for your class for a specific assignment it is helpful to keep the following guidelines in mind.

Guideline one: The less mature the writer, the more specific the FCAs should be. For example, if students are fluent, experienced writers, the focus correction area *vivid verbs* might be appropriate. But if students have had little experience with verb choice and show less interest in improving their writing, then *three vivid verbs underlined* might encourage them to strive to meet the FCA. Similarly, for the immature writer who needs explicit instruction, *three examples from text* might be more appropriate than *sufficient support*. For mature writers, *sentence variety* might be enough guidance; but with a basic writer, *at least one short sentence* (ten or fewer words) and *one medium sentence* (eleven or more words) might be a more appropriate FCA because the outcome is defined very specifically. With time and training, the focus correction area could change to simply *sentence variety*. (Note: This idea will be expanded in Chapter Five.)

Guideline two: If possible, FCAs should encourage better writing rather than simply require the student to avoid errors. For example, *no fragments* is an appropriate FCA for a very basic writer. As the writer matures, *no fragments* and *no run-ons* becomes appropriate. Later, when the student has learned to identify and avoid fragments and run-ons, *complete sentences* is more appropriate. Ultimately, *sentence variety* is the target FCA because it encourages the student to vary the length and type of sentences to produce a more mature style.

Guideline three: FCAs are best when mixed for content, organization, conventions, and style. A mix of FCAs sends two important messages to the student. First, a mix tells the student that good writing is more than no convention errors. Second, it requires the student to examine the assignment from different perspectives. For example, an assignment that requires *two compelling reasons with factual support*, a *conclusion that sums up the paper*, and *correct spelling and use of at least ten technical terms* requires the student to revise and edit in substantial ways. Capital and possessive errors, awkward sentences, and factual inaccuracies all might be evaluated because editing for the original FCAs requires careful scrutiny of the work. The right combination of FCAs becomes a set of criteria much larger than the individual focus correction areas, guiding

When assigning points to FCAs, make the points for each FCA a multiple of the number of items required by the FCA. For example, three key points should be worth 60 points or 45 points, not 50 points. It makes grading easier and more understandable. **Tip!**

students through a very careful reading of their texts.

A basic formula for creating FCAs is as follows:

- **Begin with a content FCA.** For example, explain correct steps in order; create a problem with a solution; two to three reasons with support; eight to ten facts about; three to four differences between, etc.

- **Consider a specific FCA for vocabulary.** If you want students to embed new, technical vocabulary words in their writing, you may ask students to use ten of twenty vocabulary words, spelled correctly, boxed and numbered in the margin. This FCA is very explicit and easy to grade and should be written as:

10 of 20 vocab. sp.#

Having students number the words in the margin and box or circle them on the page ensures that they have checked for correct use of technical vocabu-

---

Tip!

When introducing a focus correction area that may be new, confusing or difficult for your students (for example, thesis statement, reasons with support, paragraphing), the following four steps can help.

Step One—Focus Teaching: Introduce the focus correction area by giving a Type One assignment asking students to define it and give an example. You might ask: "What do you think a thesis statement is and give an example of one." When students share what they have written you will be able to access their prior knowledge and determine if their understanding of the FCA is different from your own. Using whatever materials you have at hand (textbooks, worksheets, examples from published work, etc.), teach the meaning of the FCA and periodically give Type Two assignments to determine if the students can correctly define the FCA and give appropriate examples.

Step Two—Focus Practice: Using papers that the students have previously written, usually from their writing folders, have students find examples of the FCA or find places where the FCA was missing or in error and have students edit directly on their past papers. This step helps make the transfer from knowing to using. For example, if your FCA is effective paragraphing, you will need to teach what this means, at least in your classroom, and then ask students to edit past papers for effective paragraphing.

Step Three—Focus Assigning: In some classes where I have modeled the Collins Writing Program, teachers skip _Step One—Teaching_ and _Step Two—Practicing_ and jump to _Step Three—Assigning_, assuming the students understand what the FCA means. This can be a mistake because the students usually have some understanding of the FCA, but it can be different from the teacher's understanding. For example, some students believe that you cannot have a one sentence paragraph or that all paragraphs must be five sentences or that all paragraphs must start with a topic sentence. When you are sure that there is a common understanding of the FCA and the students have had some opportunities to apply their understanding to their own past writing, it is time to assign the FCA on a Type Three or Type Four paper. When assigning a difficult FCA, it is usually wise to do it in the context of a Type Four assignment where the students have the benefit of peer reviewers to help out.

Step Four—Focus Correcting: In this stage, the teacher finds out how effectively the lesson has been taught and the students find out how effectively they have applied the FCA in an actual assignment. Don't skip Steps One and Two. You may be amazed at the wide range of interpretations for an FCA or, more commonly, that students can define the FCA but not apply it.

lary. It also helps the teacher evaluate the work more efficiently. Adjusting the number of vocabulary words required for mature and immature writers can help set reasonable standards for students of various maturity levels.

● **Add one FCA in the area of mechanics or conventions:** complete sentences, spelling (or no more than a specified number of spelling errors), legible handwriting, and correct capitalization are especially appropriate FCAs for students who need to pay attention to the basics of writing.

Format for Type Three Writing: Type Three writing requires a special heading for the paper, with the focus correction areas listed on the left-hand side of the top one, two or three lines. Name and date go on the top two lines on the right-hand side. Papers are numbered in the top center so that they can be filed in order for future reference. The fifth line down is the title or topic statement line. As always, students should skip lines in the body of their text (or double-space if using a computer).

```
                                    17.

   Step-by-Step Organization 50              Pat Bales
   Two examples 40                           5/29
   Attention getting beginning 10

             Title: Finding Prime Numbers
```

Schools/teachers who have been using the Collins Writing Program have found that this heading is important. It requires students to clearly document what areas or skills are required on each piece of writing, reminds students and the teacher of the requirements, and also tells an outside reader (parent, administrator, etc.) what skills the paper should demonstrate. And, because the heading is consistent from year to year, it is timesaving—it does not have to be taught fresh every year—and symbolic—it reminds students that they are in a program that continues from year to year.

Form: Type Three writing can take any form, from essay to letter to story. If the writing assignment calls for a special form (e.g., business letter), then it is usually helpful to make the elements of that particular form one of the focus correction areas (e.g., six parts of a business letter).

Audience: The primary audience for Type Three writing is the student, who will read it out loud to himself, and the teacher, who will read it and evaluate it based on the FCAs. For some assignments, the student will be asked to write for other audiences—for example, newspaper readers, students in lower grades, or school administrators. Chapter Two discusses writing for different audiences in detail.

Evaluation: The evaluation criteria for Type Three writing are the same three questions that students use to evaluate and revise their work: 1) Did I complete the assignment? 2) Does the composition sound right? Is it easy to read? 3) Do I have problems with the focus correction areas? Because the student's grade is based solely on the focus correction areas, the teacher evaluates the first two questions by simply answering "yes" or "no." If the answer to the first two questions is not "yes," then the paper is returned to the student marked as a failure or incomplete, depending on overall criteria and classroom procedures. If the answer is "yes," then the paper is accepted and the criteria of the focus correction areas applied. Depending upon the amount of time and effort required, most Type Three assignments are evaluated as quizzes or tests.

Type Three writing demands a disciplined and skilled teacher. In particular, the teacher needs classroom and time management skills and the ability to select and state the focus correction areas for each assignment and to organize the timing of the assignment to permit oral reading and editing. When giving an assignment, the teacher must explain the assignment, state that it is a Type Three, and then state the focus correction areas. As soon as the students hear the focus correction areas and, ideally, see them written on the board, they write them down on the top one to three lines of the left-hand side of their papers, with their names and date on the opposite side.

When assigning point values to the focus correction areas (for example, 50 points for ten underlined facts about the subject, 20 points for correct spelling of vocabulary words, etc.), the teacher should state the point values along with the focus correction areas and have students list the points beside each focus correction area on their papers (see Example, page 31). After this introduction, everyone in the class will know exactly what is required in the assignment.

Before giving the assignment, the teacher will have had to determine whether students will have time within a single class period to write, read out loud, and revise, or whether the first draft should be completed as homework. Especially when students are new to this approach, oral reading and revision should be done in class to guarantee that students actually do read their papers out loud to themselves and revise as needed.

Students can revise and edit directly on their papers and still have compositions that are relatively neat and easy to read because they will make their edits in the space available above or below the skipped lines. The teacher then collects and evaluates the papers in terms of the focus correction areas (providing the paper is readable and completes the given assignment). The amount of time needed to process this set of papers is limited to the time it takes to evaluate the focus correction areas.

Because the student has placed a written record of the criteria on the paper itself and because Type Three writing is evaluated *only* in relation to these criteria, points or grades or comments can be written directly beside the student's listing of the criteria on the top of his/her paper. In this way each student can see why the paper received the evaluation it did. Both teacher and student have an accurate record regarding the criteria for success.

One effective use of Type Three writing is to have students display understanding of a complete unit that introduced specific vocabulary and new, factual information. In science, the unit might be on a system of the body; in social studies, the First World War; or in math, finding the lowest common denominator. For example, imagine that an eighth grade class has just completed a unit on Siberia. The teacher might assign the following essay and focus correction areas: "Assume that a member of the class was absent for our unit on Siberia. Please write a ten- to twenty-line essay about Siberia that could be a study guide for your classmate. Here are the focus correction areas: First, tell two to four facts about the culture, geography, and about some of the problems facing Siberia, and this will be worth 60 points. Write on the first line of your paper on the left-hand side, 'culture/geography/problems/60.' Second, correctly use and spell at least 6 vocabulary words related to Siberia for 30 points; I will take off 5 points for each incorrect use or misspelling of the words on our vocabulary list on Siberia, up to 6. Write on the second line on the left-hand side of your paper, 'vocabulary words, spell/30.' Third, use complete sentences, 10 points; I will take 5 points off for each of the first two sentence fragments or run-ons. Write on the third line, 'complete sentences/10.'"

If the assignment is to be completed during class time, the teacher will have to predict how long it will take for most students to finish the first draft and then add some time for oral reading, revising, and editing. Five minutes before the time for the first draft is about to run out, the teacher will announce, "Five minutes." A one-minute warning is also appropriate.

How do I get my students to take the revision/editing process seriously? They want to dash something off and truly believe it's as good as it can get.

FAQ

ANSWER: Getting students to take revision and editing seriously is a common problem. My first response is to encourage—no, demand—oral reading of papers. Have students read papers out loud to themselves in a "one-foot" voice. This technique, coupled with skipping lines, usually produces changes that are easy to make because there is space without turning the paper into a complete mess. Sometimes students do not edit because they simply do not want to mess up their papers.

When the time for the first draft of the Type Three is complete, *all* students read their first drafts out loud to themselves simultaneously in a soft voice. When this step is complete, the students have the remaining time to edit for the three assigned FCAs, (culture/geography/problems of Siberia, correct use of vocabulary words, and complete sentences). The papers are then collected and evaluated on the FCAs. For assignments that require more writing time than is available during class, the first draft might be done at home or started in class and finished at home and revised in class on the following day, at least until students are so accustomed to oral reading and editing that they can complete these steps on their own as homework.

Example C on page 31 is a completed example of this process, with a specific grade based on the criteria. While this process is extraordinarily effective, it requires a step-by-step approach so that students use it consistently. After awhile, the process becomes automatic.

But beyond resistance due to laziness and carelessness, I find that most students do not edit or revise because they lack clarity about what to look for, and then how to fix the problem when it is found. The three-step process described here will help. I've used it countless times and find students respond really well.

After the students have completed a Type Three assignment, ask for three student volunteers to hand in the first drafts of their assignments early in the day that the assignment is due so that their drafts can be made into transparencies. I have tried photocopies of papers, but it never seems to work as well as when I use transparencies. These three papers become the samples for the class period. The students who volunteer will have the benefit of having their papers critiqued before they are "officially" evaluated by the teacher so that they can incorporate suggestions into the final draft. I tell students that volunteering their papers almost always assures a high grade. Further, when students know their papers will be displayed for the class, they tend to do their best work. These papers then serve as positive models for the rest of the class. Then, at the beginning of the class, check to see if everyone has a first draft and penalize those who do not. This is an important step because some students will not write a draft until they see the student models. This can become a major problem if student papers become plagiarized versions of the models on the overhead rather than original works.

Step One: Lead class through evaluation of first paper.

Put the first of the three student papers on the overhead and read it out loud to the class. Discuss the strengths of the paper and, being sure to involve the students, evaluate it based on the focus correction areas. I find that the process works best and is most efficient if I lead the discussion and explain the evaluation to the students.

Consider numbering the lines on the transparency as soon as you put it on the overhead. That way everyone can quickly find the place on the paper during class discussion, for example, "On line five, I think *friends* should be a

EXAMPLE C

	—*nothing on culture*
X	culture/geography/problems/ 6@ 40
	Six vocab. underlined/ 3@ 10, *two misspelled*
X	complete sentences/ 1@ 0, *two missing periods*
	(circled) 50 Joe Smith
X	5/29
X	Siberia
X	Siberia is a huge <u>tundra</u> about the size of our 50 states but
X	only the population of California. Siberia is a very diverse area.
X	Some problems facing the area is health care and education.
X	*sp–5*
X	With so few <u>indigineous</u> people (25 million) in such a large area
X	(four million) it is hard to get things to people such as books and
X	media supplies. Another problem is the horrible cold that Siberia
X	*–5*
	suffer from their is always <u>permafrost</u> because the area is above
	sp–5 ∧
	the <u>Artic</u> circle⊙ *–5*
	Siberia is a highly industrialized area. They have many gas and
	oil fields hydroelectric energy plants. I ran on coal and gold.

possessive" or "I think you could eliminate the phrase on line ten that begins the sentence."

If the assignments are long—two full pages or more—consider evaluating only the first page or sections of the paper, not the complete paper. It is important for students to see how you—the evaluator—react to different students' writing. It is equally important for you to explain your reactions and to *teach how to solve writing problems* right then and there, not just identify them.

If you discover that students are having a difficult time writing papers that meet the requirements set by the FCAs, consider stopping the process and having students practice the skill on a paper that was written previously. If students save their work in a writing folder and if these folders are kept in the classroom, they are immediately available so that students can evaluate and edit for the skill on a real paper, not on a worksheet.

When I use this process, I have students take out a specific past paper and review it for the FCA in question. If the student feels the composition needs to be revised for the FCA, the revision is done right on the actual composition. If the student feels the composition meets the requirements set by the FCA, the student does not have to change the paper but must write a short explanation about why the paper has the required skill. It has been my experience that many students demonstrate writing skills in some papers but not in others. Their application is either sloppy or random. This exercise helps students diagnose their own skill levels in a relatively painless way. It also makes every writing assignment more valuable because students never know when their papers will be used again as an editing activity. It helps if these editing exercises are collected and counted as a quiz grade.

Step Two: Have pairs of students evaluate a second paper.

Put the second paper on the overhead and read it out loud. Ask students to pair up and co-author a paragraph evaluating the paper on the overhead using the focus correction areas you have just modeled. As students are evaluating the paper, sit at the back of the classroom and evaluate the paper yourself. After a few minutes, ask if anyone would like to share his or her evaluation. This step can be made more interesting by offering extra credit to any student who comes within ten points of your grade. When I do this activity, I push it further by adding that I will take points off team members' compositions if they are off by more than ten points. This approach has a game-show aspect, but I feel that it energizes the class and keeps students from offering poorly thought-out evaluations.

Step Three: Have individual students evaluate third paper.

This step involves putting the third paper on the overhead, reading it out loud and having individual students write a short evaluation based on the focus correction areas. You and your students compare the evaluations and offer suggestions.

By the time the class has reviewed these three papers, there is a basic understanding of the assignment and what is required by the focus correction areas. By the end of this process, I have clarified the assignment and the statement of the FCAs, or I have made some adjustments in the scoring system. Students have had a chance both to watch me evaluate three papers and to influence the evaluation process. Students who volunteer their papers get an early evaluation and direct instruction on how to improve their papers, and I get practice time to evaluate papers and to clarify what I meant by the focus correction areas. Unless the three papers on overheads are quite short or the class periods long, the review of the three papers can usually take a full class period. For homework, students can then revise their papers based on the insight gained from the review of the three papers in class. The class's papers can be collected the next class, Type Three writing, or the students can do peer review, which would turn the assignment into Type Four. Although no activity is perfect, this process rarely misses because it involves all the students and helps hone their evaluation and analysis skills for an immediate task, a paper they will be handing in tomorrow.

When I explain or model this process, teachers and students usually enjoy it, but I always get comments about how time consuming it is. I would not do the three step editing process for every paper. I would do it when I was introducing a new form of writing (say, the business letter or the research paper) or new FCAs. Also, I would use the process when the assignments the students were reviewing were content rich. If students are responding to well developed assignments about the content that is being taught, the three-step process not only teaches your assessment system and how to revise and edit, but it also helps students review content. For example, if students are writing a detailed explanation about how to solve a complex math problem or a science lab report, the three-step process helps students remember how to solve the problem or how to structure a lab report because it was reviewed three times.

Type Four Writing

DEFINITION: Type Four writing is Type Three writing that has been read out loud and critiqued by another. It requires two drafts and is the most effective and efficient of all of the types at improving writing skills.

Type Four writing is the type of writing most often represented in the *Cumulative Writing Folder Program*,* a very popular writing program first published by Collins Education Associates in 1983 and designed primarily for English and language arts teachers. Type Four writing assignments have as their primary function the production of well-written, although not publishable, work.

In Type Four writing, two students sit together once each has completed a first draft. Both students read and edit their own papers following the steps for Type Three writing, then they swap papers and listen to each other's papers being read out loud by the partner, hearing not what they thought they wrote, but what another reader actually reads, with all the hesitations, flaws, and difficulties a real reader will experience. Requiring the author to hear his or her text being read by another is the critical distinguishing factor in Type Four writing. Type Four assignments create a community of learners because students must read a partner's work out loud to the partner and then help

---

**Cumulative Writing Folders* and *Primary Cumulative Writing Folders* are available from Collins Education Associates.

the partner critique the work based on the three critical questions that were discussed in Type Three writing:

1. Did I complete the assignment?

2. Does the composition sound right? Is it easy to read?

3. Have I carefully checked for problems in the focus correction areas?

While Type Three writing is an excellent approach to writing assignments because it is so efficient, Type Four is the best approach when there is no concern by the teacher about students copying from one another. Type Four writing most closely reflects real-world writing where all writers, from journalists to poets, have their work reviewed before they release it to the critical public.

In the important study, *Writing Next*, Graham and Perin make eleven research-based recommendations to improve writing skills of middle and high school students. The eleven recommendations are in order of results of their research analysis. The first recommendation is to teach specific writing strategies (e.g., oral reading); the second is to teach summarization, and the third is to use collaborative writing. They state:

> Studies of this approach compared the effectiveness of collaborative writing with that of having students compose independently. The effect sizes for all studies were positive and large. Collectively, these investigations show that collaborative arrangements in which students help each other with one or more aspects of their writing have a strong positive impact on quality (p. 16).

Format for Type Four Writing: Type Four writing requires the same heading as Type Three, but it also requires a second, edited draft with the same heading and layout.

Our *Cumulative Writing Folder Program* calls for Type Four writing. In this program, teachers follow all the steps outlined here *and* have students also keep Type Four papers in a folder to have at hand later as practice sheets, models, and review opportunities when introducing or reviewing a skill. Because the papers in the folder were originally evaluated for only the FCAs, other errors have gone unmarked. They become a rich source of material for developing further skills.

When a teacher decides to introduce, deepen, or review a skill, students have their old papers to use as practice sheets. No matter what skill, from avoidance of run-on sentences to correct use of technical terms or sufficient factual support for a thesis statement, the teacher has past papers to use as both positive and negative models. These compositions are the best source of practice sheets students will ever have. Certainly, they are more relevant and challenging than the lessons from a grammar book.

Students can make their edits right on the composition, or if major rewriting is involved, they can rewrite only those sections needing revision. Students can clip the revisions to the original composition and return them to the folder. By the end of the year, they will be impressed to see how well they can edit compositions that they thought were perfect when they first wrote them. They will also learn what all good writers come to know: another hard look almost always improves the work!

Form: Like Type Three writing, Type Four can be in any form. I always ask the peer editor to sign the work, which tends to make students more accountable.

Audience: The primary audience for Type Four writing is the author, teacher, and the class or at least the peer editor. In Chapter Two, we will discuss the role of additional "audiences" when designing assignments.

Evaluation: Type Four writing is evaluated based on the focus correction areas. I particularly like Type Four writing when the FCAs ask students to argue or develop style or refine conventions. All of these criteria are helped by a second set of eyes and a second opinion.

Example D on page 58 is an example of a Type Four composition written by a high school senior and evaluated for the FCAs listed on the top of the paper. The composition is based on the assignment described on page 57.

 # Type Five Writing

DEFINITION: Type Five writing is of publishable quality. It can go outside the classroom without explanation or qualification. Achieving publishable quality usually requires multiple drafts, and, because of the amount of time and effort required, such writing is usually considered a major project.

Type Five writing is what some experts in the field of composition call the "ideal text." It is the piece of writing that teachers hope for but rarely get—great content with no technical errors. In fact, when many teachers think of a writing assignment—especially a major assignment that will make up a significant portion of a term's grade—they think of a Type Five assignment. The high expectations for Type Five writing are both its greatest strength and its greatest flaw. The strengths of Type Five assignments are that they convey high expectations and reflect what most teachers truly want: good ideas expressed well without error in the standard conventions of written English. And there are times when Type Five assignments are the only choice, especially when the writing will reach concerned, active readers outside the classroom. Writing that goes public should be perfect, or as perfect as possible considering the age and ability level of the student.

These grand expectations lead to the weaknesses of Type Five assignments. Given the working conditions of most teachers (limited time with too many students, limited student experience with any type of writing, etc.), the expectation for perfection is probably unrealistic. Students are students, not professionals. If they could produce perfect work, they would not need to be in school. But because so many students have had Type Five expectations drilled into them for almost everything they write, they respond with writing that is the easiest to "perfect"—short and limited, with easy words and basic sentences: no risk, no voice, no opportunity to mess up. And many teachers respond in kind by focusing the vast majority of their comments on problems of capitalization, punctuation, and spelling. The fact that many students focus on the mechanical aspects of their writing and that teachers respond to these aspects is understandable and human given the teaching and learning conditions of schools today, but this fact does not discount the reality: responses to writing at the mechanical level do little to improve a student's thinking and writing skills and take up an enormous amount of teacher time and energy.

When I talk to teachers about Type Five writing, much of the conversation ends up focusing on errors in the conventions of writing, especially punctuation errors. During these conversations, my mind always goes to thoughts of *Eats, Shoots, and Leaves: A Zero Tolerance Approach to Punctuation* by Lynne Truss. This book is described on the dust jacket as, "A book for people who love punctuation and get upset when it is mishandled." The author actually has a radio show on the BBC on punctuation. This is a book you would expect to be a perfect example of Type Five writing, at least for punctuation. But not so. When *Eats, Shoots, and Leaves* was reviewed in the *New Yorker*, the opening paragraph begins, "The first punctuation mistake in *Eats, Shoots, and Leaves* . . . appears in the dedication, where a non-restrictive clause is not preceded by a comma. It is a wild ride downhill from there!" (p. 102) The author of the review, Louis Menand, goes on to enumerate punctuation error after error, ending with "Either Truss needed a copy editor or her copy editor needed a copy editor." (p. 102) And we want the kids to be perfect!

To be genuine Type Five writing, an assignment should pass through at least a few of the other Types—for example, a Type One assignment may generate ideas that become the basis of a Type Four assignment that demands content, organization, and sentence variety; after the second draft of Type Four, it may move to Type Five for technical and copy perfection. Of course, even with all of these steps, Type Five takes time. And this is as it should be. Teachers should not assign Type Five writing unless they are committed to seeing the assignment through—right down to the time demands required to check every line and every error. And if Type Five writing, a publishable piece, is the desired outcome, then teachers must also commit to making the students revise until the writing is "publishable."

In any one year or term, a limited number of Type Five assignments should be required, and even then only if they can meet at least two of the following four conditions:

1. The writing will be read by critical readers outside the classroom.

Most student writing is never read by anyone other than the teacher. If an assignment will be read outside the classroom, especially if the audience is critical, then it could be a Type Five assignment. Examples of Type Five assignments are articles for the school newspaper, business letters, college entrance essays, or anything written for a contest or to be displayed in public, outside the school.

A question I am frequently asked in this area is, "If I intend to display student work, shouldn't the work be perfect?" The best response is, if the work is displayed outside the building, it should be as perfect as it can get, but if writing is displayed in the school building, with focus correction areas written in the upper left-hand corner, then any careful reader should be able to see the criteria by which the paper was evaluated. If a critic wants to comment on other faults, a member of the school community can explain the five types of writing assignments and point out the focus correction areas written in the student's own hand. Outside critics need to understand that professional writers use many skills and that this program teaches the skills that professional writers use, but because the students are not yet professionals they are not required to use all the skills at once.

This program holds students to high standards but limits the number of standards while the student is still learning. In my experience, this system gives the individual teacher or school the educational and political rationale needed to combat critics who only want to see what is wrong with our students.

2. The writing will be produced by students who are sufficiently motivated to produce multiple drafts.

All students need motivation to produce multiple drafts, but driving unmotivated students to produce multiple drafts can be a counterproductive use of teacher energy. Ten Type Four assignments completed in two drafts will produce more thinking and learning than five Type Five assignments of four drafts each.

3. The writing will be produced by students who are sufficiently skilled to produce multiple drafts.

An underlying assumption throughout this whole discussion of Type Five writing is that students are producing written work of some length—multiple paragraphs to multiple pages. I have made this assumption because I feel that it is unwise to ask students who have a difficult time just producing a one-page composition to then make it perfect. Type Five assignments are best for reasonably fluent writers.

In addition to basic fluency, which can be developed through many Type One and Type Two assignments, students need revision skills beyond checking for spelling and capital letters. The best way to teach revision skills is through Type Three and Type Four assignments, where the focus correction areas promote revision for organization, sentence variety, word choice, elaboration, and other appropriate writing and thinking skills.

4. **The writing will be created under conditions that make publishable writing possible; that is, there is enough time for self and peer review, with oral reading, teacher feedback, and multiple revisions.**

With the exception of very short pieces, this condition limits the number of Type Five writing assignments that can be required in a year. One or two Type Five assignments of reasonable length per semester is a realistic goal for students who are fluent writers and have strong revision skills. I realize that this limit might sound as if I am suggesting low expectations for our students. Nothing could be further from the truth. I want to see students working very hard, but I also want to see them developing thinking and writing skills for their efforts, not simply improving their ability to recopy or retype. This is why I am such a supporter of Type Three and Type Four writing. Type Three and Type Four writing assignments hold students to clear standards, but because teachers can process them so much faster than Type Five, they can demand more writing and therefore provide students with more practice opportunities and more specific feedback on strengths and weaknesses—in effect, the essence of good teaching.

Teachers must try to balance their own need for students to produce "perfect" papers with the amount of teacher and student time, motivation, and energy it takes to achieve this aim. Is it really necessary to make a student redo a paper to correct two spelling errors and a possessive error if she or he has already revised the work in significant ways? I say no—unless the paper will be read by a critical outside audience.

Format for Type Five Writing: Type Five Writing is in the format required by the "publishing agency" even if the work is not going to be published. In most cases this format is typed double-spaced.

Form: Like Type Three and Type Four, Type Five can be in any form.

Audience: The audience for Type Five writing is the world outside the classroom and school, the critical outside world.

Evaluation: Type Five writing requires evaluation of all aspects of the text from content, to organization, to voice, to sentence variety, to word choice, to spelling and mechanics.

Spandel and Stiggins in *Creating Writers* (Longman, 1990) have developed six scales to evaluate writing. They include scales for ideas and content, organization, voice, word choice, sentence fluency, and conventions. More recently, these scales have been published in *6 + 1 Traits of Writing* by Ruth Culham with an added trait of presentation. Together these scales represent the traits most evaluators look for in Type Five writing. The problem is that even well-educated adults find it difficult to score high on all scales simultaneously. (How much voice does your writing have?) Nevertheless, the scales are very well thought-out and are excellent teaching tools to explain what these traits mean and how they can be developed. With them, a teacher could evaluate a Type Three assignment for ideas/content and organization and then, after time has passed, turn the same assignment into a Type Four and evaluate it for voice, word choice, and sentence fluency; and finally, use the same assignment as a Type Five work and evaluate it for all the standard conventions of publishable writing. In this way, both the student and the teacher are focused, and the teacher is never faced with the impossible task of fairly evaluating student writing with perfection as the criterion.

When I discuss the Five Types of Writing one of the most common questions is, "What about spelling?" Spelling can become a lightning rod that attracts all the energy in the room. Here is how I respond to, "What about spelling?" *For Type One writing, spelling never counts.* Placing an emphasis on spelling defeats the purpose of Type One writing, which is to quickly capture unedited ideas and questions. *For Type Two writing, spelling never counts except in very limited, announced situations.* For example, if a teacher wants to ask students to use technical vocabulary in context, the Type Two assignment might be phrased: "Use five of these eight vocabulary words about the digestive system in a short paragraph. Use the five words in such a way as to show you know the meaning. Spell the five words correctly." In this example, the words must be used *and* spelled correctly.

Type Three and Type Four writing provide many options. I prefer to use correct spelling as an FCA on Type Four rather than Type Three assignments because the peer editing process in Type Four provides the extra set of eyes so necessary to catch spelling errors. Correct spelling could be an FCA, especially if students have time to edit and have access to a dictionary. Or, a less demanding FCA could be "No more than two spelling errors per page," or some other reasonable standard. In this case, the teacher would mark every error but take off points only after the second error. Another approach is to have spelling as an FCA, but limited to words that have been identified and taught. To expedite this approach, I have included two misused/misspelled word lists in the back of this book. List I is basic, List II more advanced. I chose these words after reviewing many studies and lists. Because there is no perfect list for all classrooms or schools, I have included blank spaces so that the lists can be customized to fit individual needs. For example, a math teacher might want to add commonly misspelled words in mathematics. An FCA of "List I" or "Lists I and II" could be assigned. Misused or misspelled words from the list would be penalized, other misused/misspelled words would not. This approach encourages the basic literacy that everyone wants without penalizing students for trying to enrich their writing by using words beyond their spelling skill level. We find that this is a reasonable compromise that most faculties can live with. If the Type Three or Type Four paper is going to be revised into a Type Five (publishable) piece, then spelling can be put off until the final edit. *Of course, in Type Five writing, spelling, and all other conventions, must be correct.*

FAQ

What about the uncorrected errors? How will students learn if we do not tell them where they are wrong?

ANSWER: If we were tutors, not teachers, I would recommend that we tell the individual student, one-to-one, about the mistakes, then I would recommend we immediately teach how to fix the problem, and I would watch for body language that tells us when the student has had enough. But we are not tutors—we have classes, not individual students. Conferencing is great but is not a reasonable way to give feedback to one hundred plus students with the frequency they need.

In the real world of teaching, some students do not want extensive feedback. They are overwhelmed by it or simply do not want it, and therefore, the time we take to give it is wasted. Also, many mistakes are one time only (a missed comma here, an incorrect capital there) in an otherwise competent paper. Focus correcting gives the student exactly that—focused correction—not extensive correction. We limit feedback not because we want to keep negative information from our students, but because we have too many students to act as tutors and because we are concerned that too much feedback can be as damaging as too little.

By limiting error identification and by keeping papers in folders, we provide an opportunity to reuse the paper at a later time, after instruction, so the students can find the errors. Past papers used as practice sheets have real relevance to the student because they are the student's actual writing. I know teachers who stamp "Work in Progress" on Type Three and Type Four papers to clearly communicate that the paper is still far from perfect. Don't forget, we have Type Five writing as an option when the writing must be error free. But error free writing requires extensive feedback and large class sizes make these opportunities rare. Students need the opportunity to practice new skills frequently, with occasional demands for perfection.

It is important to note that Type Three and Type Four writing does require the teacher to indicate errors in the FCAs. When commenting on these errors, consider using the Revision and Editing Symbols on page 43. As I travel the country, I find teachers who have developed idiosyncratic systems undecipherable by anyone but themselves. How about using a common set of symbols, the same as used by professional copy editors? I have made the Revision and Editing Symbols standard page size to be easily copied and distributed. I have also added a star (∗) symbol to indicate a positive reaction. Students will be more willing to review papers if we add some positive with the negative. ▓

How does the Collins Writing Program work with students who are writing on the computer?   FAQ

ANSWER: The short answer is that the program works well with computers. When I work with students in computer labs or office-like work stations, I use the various types of writing in the same ways I would if I were in a conventional classroom. I use Type One and Type Two writing to get students to predict, to activate prior knowledge, to reflect, to recall, to compare—just as I do in any class. The only difference is that students are keyboarding their thoughts instead of handwriting them. I even have them set up their papers the same way: type of writing or FCAs listed at the top left of the document page, name and date at the top right, double-spaced.

There are a couple of special considerations that teachers should make when students are composing (Type Three or Type Four writing) on the computer. Teachers might be more demanding of students about the conventions of writing—even if there are not specific FCAs related to these areas. Since the word processing technology assists with spelling, basic grammar, and mechanics, the writer should be expected to take advantage of those aids.

Another consideration relates to the oral reading strategy. I always recommend that writers do their oral reading from hard copy rather than from the screen. One goal of the oral reading strategy is to give authors an opportunity to hear their composition as a whole and to determine if it makes sense and flows smoothly. That is most effectively done by reading all the way through without stopping to fix things. When doing the oral reading from the monitor screen it is hard to resist the temptation to stop and immediately make a change that is needed. This read/stop/fix approach works fine for editing; however, it is not conducive for identifying weaknesses in content, organization, or voice.

That is the short, tactical answer to the computer question. But the larger, strategic question of Collins Writing and computers is an important one. Computer use is pervasive in our society. A recent U.S. Department of

Education survey (Debell, 2005) indicated that 91% of students from third to twelfth grade regularly use computers. Today's students will do the vast majority of their writing—in school, at home, on the job—on the computer.

Since so much of our emphasis in the Collins Writing Program is on the thinking, planning, and refining aspects of writing, word processing is an invaluable tool of efficiency for writers. Word processed text is easy to read and easy to manipulate. With a minimum of training, even the youngest writers can word process faster than they can write by hand.

Perhaps the biggest advantage of word processing over handwritten text is the ease with which it can be changed. Changing handwritten text can be tedious and laborious for many students. Because computers make changing and manipulating text so easy, writers are actually motivated to peruse their drafts for corrections and improvements. Multiple drafts can be done quickly and with little manual effort. In the meta-analysis on writing instruction summarized in *Writing Next,* word processing was found to have a consistent positive effect on writing quality—especially for low-achieving writers. The sooner and more often we ask students to word process their writing the better.

If you need further evidence of the importance of our students making effective use of computers, read Chapter 7 of Tom Friedman's best-selling book, *The World Is Flat.* He makes the case convincingly that we need to graduate students who are as technologically savvy as possible to compete in a global marketplace. And we are not just talking about computer fluency for the elite. Computer fluency is important for non-professionals, as well. In their book, *Teaching the New Basic Skills,* Murnane and Levy make the point that the ability to use a computer effectively is a fundamental skill that human resource directors of high wage-paying companies look for in their non-degreed job candidates. Being able to use the computer effectively to compose should be part of every student's skill set.

Beyond word processing, I see a vast array of technology tools used effectively by teachers in their writing instruction. Teachers use Smart Boards to analyze models of student writing and to teach revising skills. They use software programs that teach keyboarding skills and assist with concept mapping before students draft essays. They are even using online artificial intelligence that scores and offers comments on student essays—within seconds. None of this technology, however, trumps the personal interaction of a student with a teacher. In fact, much of the research shows that the teacher's role is still critical. For example, a recent controlled study (Schwab, 2007) found that the greatest gains in writing were made by sixth graders who received feedback on their compositions from teachers in conjunction with the feedback from a sophisticated artificial intelligence program. While no substitute for human interaction, it is undeniable that these technological tools can greatly enhance our writing instruction. ▪

REVISION and EDITING SYMBOLS

Notes on Editing and the Collins Writing Program

The Collins Writing Program has five types of writing, but in Types One and Two, teachers typically do not comment on problems of mechanics or conventions; therefore, editing symbols are not needed. In Types Three and Four, editing comments are usually limited to the areas covered by the focus correction areas (FCAs). In Type Five, teachers act as true editors, helping students produce an error-free paper.

The symbols listed below are standard symbols used by editors with the exception of the ✻ which indicates a positive comment. Don't forget the ✻. Everyone likes to know the positive!

∧	Insert	**frag.**	Sentence fragment
¶	Paragraph	?	Hard to understand
ℛ	Delete	**W.C.**	Incorrect word choice
≡	Capitalize	✻**voice**	Strong voice
/	Lowercase, not a capital	✻**lead**	Good beginning
sp	Spelling	✻**close**	Strong conclusion
rs	Run on or fused sentence	✻**detail**	Good detail

General Guidelines for Teachers Using Five Types of Writing Assignments

▶ Post the definitions of the Five Types of Writing in a conspicuous place or places in the classroom.

▶ Always tell students what type of writing they will be doing, and for Type Three and Type Four, announce the focus correction areas.

▶ Have students label Type One and Type Two assignments as such on the top line, left-hand side of the paper. Type Three and Type Four will have focus correction areas on the top left-hand side. Type Five needs no label. It should, by definition, stand alone without need for qualification.

▶ Skip lines for all body text on Type One through Type Four.

▶ Do as many Type Four assignments as possible. More skill development takes place at that level than at any other.

▶ Do not drop the oral reading component from Type Three and Type Four assignments. Requiring students to listen to their own work is the best single way to improve a draft.

▶ Mix FCAs for style, content, organization, and mechanics in Type Three and Type Four assignments.

▶ Define and teach FCAs before assigning them. (Past papers in a folder are great practice sheets before students have to use new FCAs in new writing assignments.)

▶ Change FCAs to meet individual student needs.

▶ Limit the number of Type Five papers you assign and try to have them grow out of Type Three and Type Four assignments.

Advantages and Disadvantages of Each of the Five Types of Writing

TYPE ONE

Advantages

- ▶ Spontaneous—requires little preparation by teacher
- ▶ Takes little class time to complete
- ▶ Very easy to evaluate; produces effort or participation grade
- ▶ Provides opportunity for all students to stop and think—to review prior knowledge, develop questions, and think critically
- ▶ When used before instruction, provides opportunity for teacher to assess student knowledge and make decisions about what to teach
- ▶ Special advantage to quiet, less verbal students
- ▶ Promotes writing fluency

Disadvantages

- ▶ Does not directly improve specific writing skills (sentence variety, organization, word choice, etc.)

TYPE TWO

Advantages

- ▶ Spontaneous—requires little preparation by teacher
- ▶ Quick assessment of student knowledge resulting in quiz grade
- ▶ Promotes active learning by requiring students to produce information rather than simply identify information produced by others (e.g., objective test)
- ▶ Promotes content-rich writing
- ▶ Promotes writing fluency

Disadvantages

- ▶ Does not directly improve specific writing skills (sentence variety, organization, word choice, etc.)

TYPE THREE

Advantages

▶ While more time consuming than Types One and Two, very efficient

▶ Relatively easy to evaluate and grade—test or quiz grade based on mastery of three FCAs

▶ Excellent preparation for essay tests, state competency tests, etc.

▶ Improves writing skills through frequent writing opportunities, oral reading, and FCAs

▶ Helps student organize and connect content knowledge

Disadvantages

▶ Student does not receive feedback on errors other than the FCAs.

TYPE FOUR

Advantages

▶ Produces fair, objective evaluations

▶ Promotes sharing and exchange of ideas, insights, and information

▶ Creates a community of learners

▶ Produces most improvement in writing and thinking skills

Disadvantages

▶ Time consuming: peer editing/oral reading can double the amount of class time necessary to complete Type Four versus Type Three

TYPE FIVE

Advantages

▶ Results in final product that everyone (student, teachers, public) can appreciate

▶ Provides opportunity to use all skills and talents to the fullest

▶ Represents real-world standards

Disadvantages

▶ Time consuming for teacher and student

▶ Demanding for teacher who usually must act as final editor

▶ Evaluation is difficult because so many criteria must be considered or evaluation is always positive because final judgment is put off until final product is of publishable quality

▶ Somewhat unrealistic because students do not have resources writers in the real world have to produce publishable writing

Creating Types Three and Four Writing Assignments

CHAPTER

2

One of the great benefits of Type One and Type Two assignments is they are easy to create. This can also be the case with many Type Threes and Type Fours that can be thought of as Type Twos with additional criteria. This chapter will discuss how to make these transitions.

Imagine a class where a teacher has assigned the explanation of how to solve a math word problem for homework. The day the assignment is due, the teacher has photocopied or made into a transparency some of the homework solutions to show the class. A straightforward Type Two assignment might be to identify two mistakes the student made in one of the sample solutions or explanations. Or, the teacher might turn this Type Two into a Type Three by adding FCAs. For example:

FCA 1: Clearly identify two mistakes (60 points)

FCA 2: Identify one positive aspect of the solution (20 points)

FCA 3: Use and circle five math vocabulary words (20 points)

The teacher would then require the students to read their written Type Threes out loud to themselves and edit for the FCAs. A perfect Type Three! Or, the teacher could give a more elaborated and formal assignment like this one:

One way to check to see if you really understand the math chapter we have just completed is to ask you to evaluate another student's work. To make this assignment more real-world and more interesting, I'm going to ask you to imagine that you are an on-line tutor, hired by the parents of the student who did the homework solution. You are being well paid, but only when you work and only if the parents think you are being helpful. (They tend to read your messages to their child.) Write an e-mail to the student you are tutoring, explaining his mistakes and noting what he did correctly. Try to be encouraging but fair. Our FCAs will be:

- ▸ Two mistakes, clearly explained (70 points)
- ▸ One or two specific things done well (20 points)
- ▸ Encouraging tone (10 points)

47

(Note: Because I imagine a math teacher giving this assignment, I want to emphasize the math FCAs by making them worth 90 points, but I also included the 10 points for the encouraging tone, hoping it would be enough to get students to use a positive voice.)

This e-mail assignment could easily be developed into a Type Four if students peer edit their papers. In fact, it could be even better if students had different homework assignments to respond to and, therefore, had to review different math homework solutions. For example, odd rows get homework assignment A, even rows, assignment B. All students study the assignments they are given and write the evaluation, read it out loud to themselves, and edit for FCAs. Then they swap with someone in an adjoining row and critique the evaluation. This will give the students a chance to self evaluate and to peer evaluate. A perfect Type Four!

If the original homework assignments selected to be evaluated are well chosen because they represent common mistakes that many students make, this activity provides a terrific chance to help students solidify and deepen their learning.

If a teacher wanted to advance it to a Type Five, the writer could become a study guide author who is showing common mistakes students make when solving this type of math problem and explaining how to avoid them (Math for Dummies). The assignment would probably begin as a Type Four but end with a Type Five to be "published" in a class study guide to be used by future students. The downside to this Type Five is that the teacher would have to copy-edit each one before they were published. It is a great gift to the students, but a lot of work for the teacher.

There is no right or wrong approach: it all depends on the teacher's goals. The Type Two assignment gets the job done—the teacher discovers if students can identify mistakes in the solution to a math problem, great! The Type Five assignment gets a different job done—it helps the student complete a worthwhile activity to a high standard. The assignment could then be compiled with other students' critiques of different problem solutions to create a booklet written by the class.

This chapter is about creating structured, elaborate Type Three and Type Four assignments that meet the criteria I see, in one form or another, in almost all state curriculum guides—that students write for different purposes, audiences, and in different forms. This chapter explains a seven-part writing assignment to meet these state goals. Before you stop reading at this point— SEVEN PARTS!—rest assured it is not as onerous as it sounds. Like most things in this world, having a clear goal (a well designed assignment) makes the task a lot easier for the students and the teacher.

The seven elements that are described in this chapter will produce a clear, unambiguous assignment that will help students write for different purposes and in different forms for different audiences. My experience has been that the act of writing a seven element assignment slows the assignment design process down, creating a more thoughtful and well-designed task. Mike Schmoker, in *Results Now*, quotes George Hillocks' research finding that "teachers spent an average of only three minutes explaining an assignment before cutting kids loose to write" (p.95). More time during the design and explanation stages is time well spent.

John C. Bean's book *Engaging Ideas* is a writing across the curriculum guide for college professors. In his book, he makes a case of giving students assignments in written, not oral, form.

> Students appreciate handouts explaining each writing assignment.
> Although some teachers give their writing assignments orally or
> place general explanations in their course syllabi, putting assignments
> on separate handouts has several advantages: (1) it meets the needs
> of sensing or concrete learners (as identified by personality invento-
> ries such as the Myers-Briggs), who comprise, according to
> Schroeder (1993, p. 22), perhaps 60 percent of our entering students
> and who seem paralyzed by vague assignments that do not specify
> what the teacher wants; (2) it gives all students something to refer
> to late at night when their class notes no longer seem so clear
> (pp. 83–84).

These are college students who need the clarity! What about our fifth graders? The seven element assignments are for the more formal assignments you want to give. These assignments prompt higher order thinking, reflecting Bloom's hierarchy (applying, analyzing, evaluating, creating) or the big ideas or the "enduring understandings" that Wiggins and McTighe refer to in *Understanding by Design*.

The seven elements include:

Element 1. A general **summary of the assignment**

Element 2. A statement of the writer's **purpose** in the assignment— to inform, entertain, persuade, etc.

Element 3. A description of who the writer is writing as—**the writer's role**

Element 4. A description of the **audience** for the work

Element 5. A description of the writing **form** or type—essay, friendly let- ter, dialogue, etc.

Element 6. The **focus correction areas**—how the work will be evaluated

Element 7. The **procedure**—steps the writer should follow

To help make the development of seven element assignments more efficient, I have included a two-page worksheet on pages 59 to 60. Teachers with whom we work tell us that it helps facilitate the assignment development process. But first, an explanation of the seven elements.

Element 1. Assignment Summary: The assignment summary gives a general statement of the assignment with three added features: it gives a context, a rationale, and a form. First it asks the teachers to provide a context for the assignment—how it fits into the unit or year. For example, a teacher may say, "Now that we are half way through our study of the Civil War, we need to stop and reflect on the options the North and South have." Or, "Now that we are at the end of the unit, it is time to pull together our thoughts." From my experience, my students did not have a sense of the pace and flow of the class unless I told them. A connection to past or future work or how the assignment will help lay a foundation for future work is most helpful. Here's an example. "We are going to be writing a series of summaries of articles this term. You'll be doing five to six summaries, and you will be using them when we begin to do our research paper in the spring."

A second component of the assignment summary is a statement of the **rationale**, why is it important. "In our school, you will be doing research and developing the ability to summarize information as an important first step to becoming a good researcher and an expert in any area." If we can't briefly explain why we are asking the student to do an assignment, then we should reconsider the assignment. By the way, one very legitimate rationale is to test student knowledge.

The final component is a brief statement about the **form** the writing will take—a letter, a poem, a poster, or a 110 to130-word summary. For example, here is an assignment summary from our seven-part vocabulary card assignment on pages 73–74.

Vocabulary Cards:
Using Cards to Master Technical Vocabulary

Project Summary: To demonstrate knowledge in a field, one must be able to use the vocabulary of that field. But your textbook introduces vocabulary a little at a time and then doesn't review it. Consequently, you may learn the vocabulary for the chapter test and never study it again! To learn and really remember, it is more effective to study frequently in short bursts than to study just once for a long time. When it comes to learning vocabulary, one of the easiest and most efficient ways is with vocabulary cards. This assignment requires that you create your own set of vocabulary cards. In fact, just creating the cards will help you begin to remember the words. Do your best. We will be repeating this assignment frequently during the year. You'll end up with an impressive collection of vocabulary cards. Also, I'll be testing on vocabulary all year long, and I will include words from the full year, not just the last unit—so don't lose your cards.

Element 2. Writer's Purpose: When completing a writing assignment, the writer should always be aware of at least one purpose. The purpose may be simple—to inform, to persuade, to entertain, or complex—to persuade while informing and entertaining. A teacher may state the purpose precisely: "Analyze this problem by developing a clearly stated thesis and providing reasons from the text to support your thesis." Or, "Explain why chlorophyll is important in plants in a way that is interesting and clear to fifth graders." Or, instruct the student to decide: "Considering the theme of individual rights and group responsibility that we have been discussing in this social studies unit, select a purpose (entertain, explain, inform, document, etc.) and create a work that reflects your purpose."

While there are many terms and categories to describe the purpose of writing, Nancy McHugh lists four domains or purposes for writing that are practical and easy to use. (See *Practical Ideas for Teaching Writing as a Process* edited by Carol Booth Olson.) These four domains give the teacher and the student a system to identify the purpose of a writing assignment that is simple enough to teach easily yet complex enough to encompass most types of writing assignments. The four domains with McHugh's definitions are listed here.

Imaginative/narrative writing: Writing in which the main intent is to tell a story.

Practical/informative writing: Writing in which the intent is to provide clear information.

Sensory/descriptive writing: Writing in which the main intent is to create a dominant impression—so that the reader has the same impression as the writer.

Analytical/expository writing: Writing in which the main intent is to analyze, explain why, in the writer's opinion, something is the way it is, or to influence or persuade.

Using the most traditional of all writing assignments, the book report and the four domains, it would be very easy to create four very different writing assignments. For the imaginative/narrative purpose, students could be asked to write a "just discovered" chapter from a novel they have been reading. For the sensory/descriptive purpose, students could be asked to write a character sketch, especially of a less-developed character, or to describe in detail a scene that the author has not fully described. For the practical/informative purpose, a student could summarize a chapter or section, create an outline of events, or write a brief biography of the author. For the analytical/expository purpose, the student could evaluate the book in any number of ways or explain why it should or should not be included in the curriculum.

Whatever the assignment, it is important to state the purpose or to be clear that the student is to decide the purpose. It is equally important to teach students to determine the purpose of every writing assignment even if their other teachers do not explicitly state the purpose. Students can be discouraged if they feel they have written well but are evaluated harshly because they missed the purpose of an assignment. For example, in a misguided attempt to be creative, a student might give a fictional account of an important event in Lincoln's life when the teacher wanted an analysis of Lincoln's political beliefs.

Element 3. Writer's Role: Most assignments assume that students will write from their own point of view, as themselves, and this assumption is usually correct. But excellent writing can be elicited by asking students to shed their own persona and assume a new one presenting their opinions, feelings, or research in the role of this assumed personality. Many times students' writing will blossom when they are free to create a new voice. I have seen tentative writers become more assertive simply by pretending to be someone else.

One of my favorite roles for a student writer, especially when the purpose of the assignment is analytical/expository or practical/informative, is to ask the student to become a textbook editor or a SparkNotes author and summarize, explain, or analyze academic content for students younger or less able than themselves.

Recently, I read a fascinating group of assignments in which students assumed the persona of Lady Macbeth's doctor. They had been asked to write the physician's journal, being true to the events in the play. "Becoming" an historical figure from a social studies unit or a fictional character in a work of literature and presenting that person's opinions is a marvelous way to help students appreciate and present issues. But new personae do not have to be human. In science, I have seen practical/informative pieces in which students had to "become" a drop of water on a leaf of a plant and document their journey to the roots. Adopting a different persona is not a rhetorical trick. For centuries, authors have used this technique to capture the imagination of an audience.

Some possible writer's roles include:

• yourself	• school administrator
• expert in field	• teacher
• friend	• scientist
• family member	• book character
• journalist	• historical figure
• textbook writer	• newscaster
• advertiser	• celebrity

Element 4. Audience: Just as students usually assume they will be writing as themselves, they also assume that the teacher is their sole audience. In reality, this is almost always the case. But students need to learn to write for different audiences. Simulating real-world audiences in writing assignments can

help students adjust their word choice, tone, organization, etc. in ways that will help them grow as writers.

My favorite audience for writing assignments is any younger, less-knowledgeable audience than the writers, e.g., fourth graders writing for second graders, seniors for sophomores. Professional writers write because they feel they know more than their audience or because they feel they have a message their audience should hear. Also, writing for less informed audiences encourages the writer to be more thorough and precise with language. Rarely, except in school, is anyone expected to write for an audience that is more experienced and knowledgeable than the writer. Writing for someone who knows more than you is a most inhibiting experience.

Audiences can be imagined. Again, using the book report as an example, an audience can be simply a class of students assigned to read the book; another audience could be the author or publisher to whom students suggest ideas for a sequel or off-shoot involving a minor character. Students could be asked to write condensed versions in the style of a *Reader's Digest* for readers who do not have the time to read the whole book or a simplified version for those who do not have reading skills as advanced as those of the students who are writing the report. In fact, all of these audiences could be real and all create a possible real-world purpose for writing.

Some possible audiences include:

- school committee member
- student at lower grade
- school administrators
- literary or historical character
- student who has missed class
- next year's class
- celebrities

- concerned citizen
- community leaders
- parent
- peers
- expert in field
- magazine readers
- contest judges

Element 5. Form: In addition to writing for different purposes and audiences and in different personae, students should write in different forms as well. Some students will respond to every assignment with a multi-paragraph essay while others are creative enough to try other possibilities—a poem, dialogue, story, or editorial. Assignments that require different forms help writers learn the elements of each form and discover their own best form. Would-be journalists should write some poetry, and poets, some essays. Returning to the book report as an example, it could take the form of advertising copy to encourage a book's sale, a book review, or a memo to the author with suggestions for improvements, additions, or deletions. The assignment should either require a specific form or help the author select a form appropriate to the purpose, audience, and persona.

Some possible forms include:

• letters to imaginary people	• diaries	• summaries
• conversations/dialogues	• children's books	• brochures
• biographies/obituaries	• slogans/mottos	• news reports
• advertisements/commercials	• displays/posters	• dialogues
• applications/resumes	• study guides	• speeches
• annotated bibliographies	• interviews	• case studies
• "personal" letters between experts	• post cards	• reviews
• encyclopedia entries	• journals	• fables
• fact sheets	• eulogies	• plays
• reviews	• memos	• tests

Element 6. Focus Correction Areas (FCAs): The focus correction areas tell the writer what the evaluative criteria will be. FCAs are explained in detail in the section on Type Three writing in the previous chapter and in my book *Selecting and Teaching Focus Correction Areas.* One reminder though—try to mix FCAs for style, content, and organization and resist the temptation to over-emphasize mechanical FCAs.

Element 7. Procedure: This final element, procedure, provides students with the steps that will lead them to complete the assignment. Instructions may be highly structured, requiring students to complete certain steps before continuing on to the next, with deadlines for each part. The procedure section is where activities such as graphic organizers, class discussions, and review of notes are highlighted. An elaborate procedure section may lead students through the prewriting, drafting, and revising phases. Or, they may contain only a few guiding questions or suggestions to follow or not.

It is in the procedure section that the teacher can remind students about choices they have to make. "Select the best form for your message—memo, friendly letter, business letter, note, etc." In addition, this is the best place to remind students of due dates. "First draft is due Thursday at the beginning of class." In general, the more complex or innovative the assignment, the more detailed the procedure section needs to be.

One intended outcome for this type of structure is to help students become aware of the planning it takes to accomplish writing assignments and to internalize the structure for other assignments when the teacher does not provide as much guidance. As students become more familiar with the process, they should require less structure; nevertheless, written due date, guiding questions, and reminders about decisions that need to be made are always helpful, even for the most able and mature students.

The assignment on page 57 is an example of a Type Four assignment developed according to the system described in this chapter. It was developed for a science class of high school students who had finished studying the Periodic Table. Example D, page 58, provides a sample response that has been evaluated based on the FCAs.

In the graded Example D, the student made two errors in the third FCA (correct caps, commas and end marks) and lost all ten points. These are FCAs the teacher assigned, and because they were written in the assignment, they were clear to the student. My guess is that because the teacher was a science teacher, not an English teacher, there was a limit to how many points could be lost for an "English" skill. On a personal note, I like what this teacher did. The ten points should be enough to encourage a close proofreading of the paper to avoid errors in capitalization, commas and end marks. The student who wrote Example D missed two errors and lost ten points according to what the FCA said the penalty would be. The teacher also felt that the student demonstrated a good understanding of the Periodic Table and awarded almost full credit—eighty points.

On pages 59–60 we have provided a worksheet that makes creating elaborated Type Three and Type Four assignments easier. You may want to make multiple copies to use when you get a good idea for an assignment. From my own experience, filling the worksheet out always helps me clarify what I want and helps me stop and think about alternative audiences, forms, and writer's roles that did not immediately come to mind.

Over the last few years, I've added the section "Optional FCAs to accommodate or challenge students" to the worksheet. I have found that if I stopped to think about modifying the FCAs for some students (fewer or more vocabulary words, change number of reasons, or focus on specific error of convention, etc.), I could make the assignments more accessible or demanding for select students.

Tip!

The most commonly asked question about every writing assignment is, "How long?" For some students, "Long enough to do the job" is not enough guidance. If immature writers need a clear indication of length—a goal to shoot for—then I suggest providing a response in a number-of-written lines form. For example, "Your memo will probably run twenty to thirty written lines." Now the student has an idea about length but is not locked into a number of paragraphs, sentences, or words. Students are then free to structure the assignment in a way that makes sense to them, for example, many short paragraphs with fewer, longer, more detailed sentences. With this type of instruction, the students will still have a sense of magnitude of the final product.

In my workshops, teachers sometimes balk at my suggestion of a clear length requirement, but as I spend more time in the "real world," I find that length requirements, or at least suggestions, are attached to almost all writing jobs, whether it be a three act play (get the audience out in 2 to 2-1/2 hours), a newspaper column (800 to 1,000 words), or a proposal for a grant (no longer than 10 single spaced pages, size twelve font). If the length requirement is well thought-out by the teacher, it makes the assignment more authentic.

But I found I would more likely make these modifications if I noted them while I was planning the assignment.

My new guideline to myself is that for every time I modify the FCA to make it easier for a struggling student, I try to make it more demanding for another more able student. For example, if the class needs to include eight to ten facts about a topic in an informational piece of writing, then some select students may only have to include five to seven, but others may have to include twelve to fifteen. Of course, this approach is up to the teacher. For some assignments (for example, those that count as a major test), all students would have the same standard. But, as we all know, many students are capable of producing better work if they know the expectations and if the expectations are clear. In fact, top students appreciate being held to a higher standard if the teacher has a positive relationship with them and explains why the standard is higher. "I know you want to go to a top college and these are the types of standards you need to meet in order to succeed at a top school."

Explaining the Periodic Table

1. Assignment Summary	Now that we have finished studying the Periodic Table, your job is to put the information you have to use. This assignment requires you to imagine yourself as a textbook writer for a middle school science text. Your assignment from the publisher is to write a 300- to 350-word description of the Periodic Table. Also, the editor has reminded you of a difficult problem. Science books have been criticized for not having enough solid information, but they must be written so that middle school students can understand them and not be confused; therefore, you must have solid information that is easy to understand.
2. Purpose	The purpose of this assignment is to be informative. You are to write clearly, providing information that will help a middle school student understand what the Periodic Table is and why it is important.
3. Writer's Role	You will be writing as if you were a science textbook writer.
4. Audience	Write for students in grades six, seven, or eight.
5. Form	Create a multi-paragraph textbook selection, no more than 350 words. Assume that your readers will have the Periodic Table printed in the textbook.
6. FCAs	▶ Describe what the Periodic Table is and why it is important. (45 points) ▶ Explain how to use the Periodic Table. (45 points) ▶ No capital, comma or end mark errors. (10 points—5 off each error, up to 2)
7. Procedure	☐ Review your notes and textbook to determine if you feel you have enough information to describe the Periodic Table and why it is an important scientific tool. If you feel you need more information, you can interview classmates and/or research the Periodic Table in the library. ☐ Write a Type Three essay, due on _____. ☐ In class on _____, you will peer edit your Type Three essay following our standard procedure. For homework that night you will recopy, including revisions. The Type Four essay is due the next day.

EXAMPLE D

More detail on how to use, less history

7.

Chris English
10/20

Describe P. T. and its importance – 45 pts. 45
How to use P. T. – 45 pts. 35
Correct caps, commas, and end marks – 10 pts. 0

Title: Periodic Table

More than a 150 years ago, a Russian scientist named Mendeleev was investigating the 63 chemical elements that had been discovered at that time. Mendeleev became convinced that there had to be a certain pattern among these elements. Despite the *missing period –5* fact that the many elements varied from rare and valuable solids to strange and deadly gases, Mendeleev knew there must be a way to group the elements according to their properties.

So Mendeleev made a notecard for each of the 63 known elements. On the card he listed the atomic mass, density, color, melting point and valence (bonding ability) for each element. He noticed that if all the cards were arranged in order of increasing atomic mass, the valence numbers always appeared in the pattern 1234321. Even more remarkable, Mendeleev observed that if the cards were arranged in rows of seven, all the elements in each column showed similar properties, and the same valence!

To explain this discovery, Mendeleev stated that "the properties of the elements are periodic functions of their atomic masses." Used this way, the word periodic means "repeating according to some pattern."

Caps –5 The periodic table is an important tool for scientists because a great deal of information about the elements can be gathered very quickly. As you read, refer to your copy of the periodic table.

Each square on the table refers to one of the 109 known elements. In each square the following information is given: its atomic number, chemical symbol, name, and atomic mass. In addition to the information presented in each square, the elements are also grouped into certain vertical columns (called families) and horizontal rows (called periods), which will provide key information about the element. All of the elements in Family 1A, for instance, are silver-white shiny metals. And the pattern of every period will always be the same: a very active solid (such as potassium in Period 4) moving gradually to a very inactive gas (such as krypton in Period 4). By using the periodic table correctly, both scientist and student alike can quickly gather information about all of the world's elements.

Create a Seven Element Writing Assignment Worksheet

Subject _____ Class _____ Date _____

**Assignment Summary
and Rationale**

Writer's Purpose(s)	*Analytical/Expository* • *Practical/Informative* *Sensory/Descriptive* • *Imaginative/Narrative* Persuade • Inform • Describe • Entertain • Multi Purposes

Writer's Role	Yourself Teacher Family member Historical figure School administrator	Book character Textbook writer Expert in field Scientist Journalist	Friend **Other:**	
Audience	Student at lower grade Next year's class School administrator Student who has missed class	Expert in field Magazine readers Concerned citizen School committee member	Parent **Other:**	
Form	Study guide Diary Song/Rap Children's book Advertisement Job description Explanation Advice column Collection for future classes	Journal Bumper sticker Obituary Slogan/Motto Interview News report Application Wanted poster Post card	Editorial Definitions Biography Summary Directions Letter Memo Poem Retelling	Email/Fax Test Play Report Brochure Fable Speech **Other:**

FCA	Pts.

FCA	Pts.

FCA	Pts.

Optional FCAs to accommodate or challenge students	Pts.

Procedures

❑ Read your report out loud in a one-foot voice. Check for any confusing parts.

❑ Edit your FCAs following your teacher's directions.

❑ Option: Type Four: Have a partner read your paper out loud to you. Get feedback on your FCAs. Write a second draft with all your improvements.

❑ Final draft due on _____.

Essential Writing Assignments

CHAPTER

3

There is nothing better than a well done, teacher-made writing assignment with seven clearly stated elements, connected directly to the content, and designed with a specific class in mind. But within this ideal, one may ask, are some assignments better than others? It turns out some are. There is a body of research that supports the merit of some assignments over others, no matter how well the teacher-made assignment is designed. My review of the research suggests there are at least four writing tasks that are essential. They include summaries, vocabulary cards, comparisons and contrasts, and persuasive essays. This chapter makes the case for the importance of each of these four assignments for all students over multiple years, and provides an example of a seven element assignment for each of the four.

▶ Essential Assignment One: The Summary

In the 2007 Carnegie Corporation's meta-analysis of research, *Writing Next: Effective Strategies to Improve Writing of Adolescents in Middle and High School*, the authors found summarization to be the second most effective strategy to improve adolescent writing skills, right after teaching explicit strategies for planning and revising compositions. They define summarization as "explicitly and systematically teaching students how to summarize texts" (p. 4). In another meta-analysis of the research, *Classroom Instruction that Works: Research Based Strategies for Increasing Student Achievement*, the authors reported similar powerful effects not just to improve writing skills but to improve overall academic achievement. Based on these two very significant studies, writing summaries has to be considered essential. (Remember, these conclusions were a result of meta-analysis, a statistical technique that combines the effects of many studies—not just one.) Bean elaborates on the value of summary writing as follows:

> Writing summaries or précis of articles or lectures is a superb way to develop reading and listening skills, to practice decentering, and to develop the skills of precision, clarity, and succinctness (Bean, 1986). In composing a summary, the writer must determine the hierarchical structure of the original article, retaining without distortion the logical sequence of its general statements while eliminating its specific details. Summary writers must also suspend their own views on a subject to articulate fairly what is often an unfamiliar or even unsettling view in the article being summarized (pp. 83–84).

Resources are available to help teach summarization. Emily Kissner's book *Summarizing Paraphrasing and Retelling* is particularly good for middle schools. Rick Wormeli's *Summarization in Any Subject* has fifty techniques for all grade levels. Frey, Fisher, and Hernandez's article "What's the Gist? Summary Writing for Struggling Adolescent Writers" is another valuable resource. I will add my "Ten Percent Summary" to the mix.

The Ten Percent Summary, written as a seven element assignment, is on pages 71–72 and asks students to summarize an original article in ten percent of the words. It works best when it is used in middle and high schools with nonfiction articles of 500 to 2,000 words, the typical length of many articles and selections on reading tests. As you will note, I have included the FCA <u>**S**</u>. **A**. "**T**". where **S** stands for the **source** of the article, usually underlined because most articles are from books, newspapers, magazines, etc.; the **A** stands for the **author**; and the "**T**" the **title**, usually in quotes. Having the students incorporate these references into the body of the summary helps them develop the academic style needed for a research paper. For example, a student could begin a summary of a newspaper article as follows:

> The <u>New York Times</u> article by John Jones "Writing Skills Declining" discusses recent research on the writing skills . . .

If students are using a computer to write their summaries, they should italicize the source (newspaper, magazine, book) rather than underline.

I have used Ten Percent Summaries many times and have always found that students jumped into the task, especially reluctant writers and students who struggle with English. For skilled writers, I usually give more demanding passages to summarize but keep the same FCAs. Another advantage of summary writing is that teachers can use one of the three FCAs to develop a writing skill (for example, sentence variety, vivid verbs, strong concluding sentences) because students do not have to focus all their energies on developing new content.

If I have convinced you that the summary is a good idea, let me also try to convince you to do many summaries, not just one or two. The benefit of this highly structured approach is that students become good at it with practice, but they usually need at least four or five summaries to be able to do them quickly and well.

▶ Essential Assignment Two: Vocabulary Cards

This assignment, like the summary and the comparison and contrast, was influenced by the research of Robert Marzano and his books *Building Background Knowledge for Academic Achievement* and *Classroom Instruction That Works*. In both books, Marzano provides detailed research on the power of direct instruction of academic vocabulary—especially to English language learners, and I encourage you to review these sources. In *Classroom Instruction That Works* he summarizes five "generalizations that can be used to guide instruction in vocabulary terms and phrases:"

▶ Students must encounter words in context more than once to learn them.

▶ Instruction in new words enhances learning those words in context.

▶ One of the best ways to learn a new word is to associate an image with it.

▶ Direct vocabulary instruction works.

▶ Direct instruction on words that are critical to new content produces the most powerful learning.

He then goes on to present a five-step process to teach new terms:

Step 1. Present students with a brief explanation or description of the new term or phrase.

Step 2. Present students with a nonlinguistic representation of the new term or phrase.

Step 3. Ask students to generate their own explanations or descriptions of the term or phrase.

Step 4. Ask students to create their own nonlinguistic representation of the term or phrase.

Step 5. Periodically ask students to review the accuracy of their explanations and representations.

The seven element assignment Vocabulary Card on pages 73–74 is my interpretation of Marzano's five generalizations and five processes. I think it is true to his process and produces a study aid (vocabulary card) that can be used over the course of a year. I had to fight with some of my associates to include this assignment. It is not that they argue against the value of a rich and precise vocabulary. Their feelings were that the assignment did not constitute enough writing—did not generate enough words—to be included as an essential writing assignment. In fact, they are correct. One vocabulary card is not much of a writing assignment, but ten or twenty, all with an illustration and an original sentence that conveys the meaning of the word, add up. Also, the assignment cannot be beat for practicality. By simply creating the cards, students will actually engage with words and by having the cards, teachers and students will have an activity to use for independent study, group work, and continued reinforcement.

Most teachers who elect to do the vocabulary card assignment will probably select the words from a current unit or theme or chapter, which makes great sense, but you also might want to cross-reference the specific words with more general academic words that we sometimes assume the students know. Averil Coxhead has created a list of 570 words that are used frequently in all academic texts regardless of the discipline but may not be taught directly. For example, some of Coxhead's most common academic words include *analyze, assess, assume, derive, indicate, respond, method, significant,* and *theory.*

While teachers know that students probably do not know the meaning of *trapezoid, tensile strength, tendon* or *tsunami* unless they are directly taught, they might not realize that their students also do not know the meaning of *interpret, policy, illustrate,* or *text.* I recommend Coxhead's website, **http://language. massey.ac.nz/staff/awl/index.shtml** as a great resource for general academic vocabulary that is not subject specific but nevertheless is critical for students to understand. You should consider incorporating general as well as specific academic words into your list for vocabulary cards.

For example, imagine a class where seventy to ninety percent of the students had almost all the required cards. (I realize one hundred percent of students is a stretch, so imagine seventy.) Also imagine a class has finished a task early, or has a substitute, or needs a break. (I'm thinking of a block schedule ninety to one hundred minute period.) Following are some activities that would take five to ten minutes and provide a great review.

1. Teacher or student shows an illustration, definition, or reads the sentence without the vocabulary word and class must give the word.

2. Students create grid of cards (3 × 3, 4 × 4, etc.) on desk with words face up. Teacher or student reads definition and students flip words over to form a row—Bingo!

3. Teacher or student gives vocabulary word. Students must define or use in a sentence that conveys the meaning of the word.

4. Teacher or student shows illustration of word and students must guess the word—a form of Pictionary.

▶ Essential Assignment Three: Comparison and Contrast

I remember once hearing that intelligence is the ability to see similarities in things that are different and differences in things that are similar. This is the essence of a comparison and contrast assignment. Comparison and contrast assignments are terrific assessments because they help the teacher determine if students can distinguish between concepts or ideas, especially when the differences are subtle. For example, distinguishing between baseball and football is easy, but distinguishing between professional football and college football is quite another task, requiring more in-depth knowledge of the game. Here are some academic examples:

> plant cells – animal cells
>
> Republicans – Democrats
>
> decimal – fraction
>
> Sparta – Athens

Marzano, Pickering, and Pollock's research in *Classroom Instruction That Works* supports summarizing as the second most effective technique to increase student achievement; identifying similarities and differences is the first! Marzano and his colleagues encourage students to identify similarities and differences through four activities: comparing, classifying, creating metaphors, and creating analogies. The essential assignment presented here focuses on the comparing activity which is made even more explicit by calling it comparing (how things are alike) and contrasting (how things are different). On pages 77–78 I have a seven element assignment, "Similar, but Different: Comparing and Contrasting When Differences Are Subtle" which provides students with a structured assignment to practice this skill. Marzano and his colleagues state:

> Although the process of comparing might seem simple, it is not. We suggest that teachers introduce the process of comparing by presenting students with highly structured tasks. This means that a teacher identifies for students the items they are to compare and the characteristics on which they are to base the comparison. These tasks, by definition, focus (even constrain) the type of conclusions students will reach. Consequently, they should be used when a teacher's goal is that all students obtain a general awareness of the same similarities and differences for the same characteristics (p. 17).

When I was field testing this comparison and contrast assignment, a well respected principal commented on it. She felt it was predictable and "pretty typical," especially the Venn diagram. I asked if I went into a sixth grade class in her school right then and asked if they could compare the fifth grade with the sixth grade (something they obviously knew well) how many would use a Venn diagram to organize their thoughts? I also wondered how many would actually write an organized essay on how the fifth grade was both similar and different from the sixth? Or, would the students write a more unfocused paper on what they liked or disliked? The principal thought for a minute and guessed that while most students know what a Venn diagram is, few would use one without prompting and fewer still would actually compare and contrast the two years in any organized way. And this is a very high achieving school.

▶ Essential Assignment Four: Persuasive Essay

If there is one assignment that has become a right-of-passage in America's middle and high schools it is the short, twenty-five to thirty minute persuasive essay. Because persuasive prompts have become the norm on state tests and appear on the SAT and ACT exams, the only truly national tests we have, they have become essential assignments. In spite of the fact that the persuasive essay has been roundly criticized for its length (much too short), topic choice (too limiting, not fair to kids of diverse backgrounds or limited experience), and because it encourages formulaic writing, it is the prompt of choice across the country.

George Hillocks provides an extensive and scathing analysis about the use of short, persuasive writing prompts in state tests in *The Testing Trap: How State Writing Assessments Control Learning.* He discusses how states' prompts, by their very nature, tend to encourage the formulaic essay. He describes the 3.55 composition (three reasons, five paragraphs, five sentences in each paragraph) taught in some schools to "help" students pass state tests. He concludes that, "In most states, the assessment must be altered if writing and thinking are to flourish" (p. 206).

In spite of the criticism, the short persuasive essay seems to be firmly established as part of the assessment process of our schools, and the ability to create a clear, cogent argument under time limits is an extremely important skill that mirrors many of the essay tests students will see in college and memos they will create when they enter the working world. Mike Schmoker, who has written extensively on how to improve our schools, writes in *Results Now* that what we need is "generous amounts of close, purposeful reading, rereading, writing and talking" (p. 53). Currently he feels our students get "the Crayola curriculum" with too much drawing, coloring, and worksheets rather than "argumentative literacy" that they need. In *Educational Leadership* he quotes Conley's study, sponsored by the Association of American Colleges and Universities:

> Argumentative literacy may be the most essential skill students need
>
> to succeed in college. The study's recurring theme is that students
>
> abandon college chiefly because K-12 education does not prepare

them to think, read and write argumentatively (Conley, 2003). Being skilled in argument equips all students—college bound or not—to become intelligent, contributing employees and citizens (p. 64).

We owe our students the opportunity to refine their persuasive writing skills so they can succeed, especially when confronted by tests. Here is an example of a prompt given by the ACT:

> Educators debate extending high school to five years because of increasing demands on students from employers and colleges to participate in extracurricular activities and community service in addition to having high grades. Some educators support extending high school to five years because they think students need more time to achieve all that is expected of them. Other educators do not support extending high school to five years because they think students would lose interest in school and attendance would drop in the fifth year. In your opinion, should high schools be extended to five years?
>
> In your essay, take a position on this question. You may write about either one of the two points of view given, or you may present a different point of view on this question. Use specific reasons and examples to support your position.

The SAT uses a slightly different approach, asking the students to "think carefully about the issue presented in the following excerpt and the assignment below:"

> We must seriously question the idea of majority rule. The majority grinned and jeered when Columbus said the world was round. The majority threw him into a dungeon for his discoveries. Where is the logic in the notion that the opinion held by a majority of people should have the power to influence our decisions?
>
> Assignment: Is the opinion of the majority—in government or in any other circumstances—a poor guide? Plan and write an essay in which you develop your point of view on this issue. Support your position with reasoning and examples from your reading, studies, experience, or observations.

A third example is from Texas' eighth grade test:

> The principal of your school is thinking of starting a program in which eighth graders would help second and third graders who are having trouble with their school work. Write a letter to your principal in which you state whether or not you think this program is a good idea. Be sure to give convincing reasons for your position and to explain your reasons in detail.

All of the tests call for a similar structure: a multi-paragraph essay with an introduction that states the writer's opinion, a body that provides reasons and details, and a conclusion that wraps up the essay with some sort of summary or call-to-action. I have read many of these essays; the worst are unclear, off topic, or fail to argue the position in any reasonable way. The vast majority usually take a clear position but develop it poorly. The best are wonders to behold, with great support, voice, metaphors and sophisticated word choice. Some students who are natural born writers will do well in spite of the school's curriculum or instructional practice. But all students can benefit from practice and coaching, especially when there is a time limit.

The fourth essential assignment, the persuasive essay, is designed to provide this practice. The FCAs have been designed to get to the single biggest problem most students have in answering persuasive prompts—compelling reasons with details. But before we can get compelling reasons with relevant details, first we need students to simply *identify* reasons.

To help develop reasons with details, the persuasive writing assignment has a "Short Persuasive Essay Focus Sheet—HELPS" on page 83 to help the student organize reasons with details and create a clear thesis. Completing this sheet may seem too time consuming for a twenty-five to thirty minute essay but, with practice, can be accomplished within five minutes, leaving twenty minutes to write the essay. The advantage with this approach is that the writer begins writing with a fully developed thesis and clear reasons and does not have to invent them while writing—the organization is in place.

The focus sheet is designed to help students think about reasons and details, especially reasons that go beyond personal feelings and incorporate knowledge from their studies and reading. I have created categories that middle and high schools students can quickly recall. The categories of reasons are organized into five groups that can be more easily remembered by using the acronym **HELPS**, where **H** stands for historical, **E** for economic, **L** for literary, **P** for personal and **S** for scientific. The categories are not mutually exclusive and they are not meant to be. Rather, they are designed to give students familiar categories to sort their ideas into and then check to see if they missed a compelling idea because of the pressure of time. A more expansive description of these reasons is explained below, but HELPS should give the students a mnemonic device to get the general categories down.

Historical, legal, and political reasons are reasons that deal with lessons from the past, established laws, and government.

Economic and resource based reasons are reasons that deal with time, money, or natural resources.

Literary and aesthetic reasons are reasons based on art, culture, and literature.

Personal, ethical, and religious reasons are reasons based on personal experience as well as ethical and religious beliefs.

Scientific reasons are reasons that can be proven through observation, the scientific method, or that appeal to known facts.

Using the ACT prompt on page 67, "Should high school be extended to five years?" I have included a focus sheet on page 70 that serves as an example of what a student might do, under time pressure, to develop and organize ideas. This focus sheet leads me to the critical idea behind all four of the essential assignments: they are designed to be done repeatedly, using the same basic procedure, so that students become facile with the process.

I wish I knew exactly how many times a student would have to do each of the four essential assignments to show marked improvement. I don't know, but my guess is that it is a lot, say five to fifteen spread over a period of a year and, best yet, over a number of subjects, and then repeated the following year to reawaken the skills that may have gone dormant over the summer.

These few essential writing assignments do not constitute a complete writing program, but they do sharpen important academic skills that include the ability to read a text and condense it in your own words; the ability to create a study aid to improve vocabulary; the ability to describe similarities and differences especially when these differences are subtle; and the ability to argue for a position. Think about your school's students. How many can do these tasks well? If the answer is that you are not sure, give the assignments a try and modify them to fit the needs of your students and your teaching style. Remember what the research states regarding their effectiveness and include these assignments into your curriculum. The more you and fellow faculty members require your students to complete them, the more quickly and effectively the students will perform.

FOCUS SHEET **Short Persuasive Essay Sheet— HELPS: Getting and Organizing Your Ideas**

REASONS FOR	REASONS AGAINST
H Historic, Political, Legal States can always change laws.	**H** Historic, Political, Legal We have always had 4 years of high school and are a great country.
E Economic, Resource Utilization Would learn more—get better jobs.	**E** Economic, Resource Utilization Would lose chance to work—make money. More would drop out, fewer with HS diploma
L Literary, Aesthetic ?	**L** Literary, Aesthetic ?
P Personal, Ethical, Religious Some kids love school Some would be better athletes—more mature	**P** Personal, Ethical, Religious You can go to community college or prep school if you feel you need to before college. I'm ready to go to college. Some kids hate HS after one year, forget four years.
S Scientific Not sure—more is not always Better Let's test	**S** Scientific Are there any studies to show a fifth year would make a difference? Untested

Position
- → Yes
- → Under certain conditions/circumstances
- → (No)

Reason 1 ___economic___
Reason 2 ___personal___
Reason 3 ___scientific___

THESIS STATEMENT: Topic / Position / 2 to 3 Reasons without "I."
 High school should not be five years for economic, personal, and scientific reasons.

The Ten Percent Summary:
Telling the Main Points of a Nonfiction Article

Project Summary	A landmark study (*Writing Next*) examined all the research on what activities help students improve their writing skills. Second from the top of the list was a surprising result: write summaries. As it turns out, writing a summary helps students read better, study more effectively, remember the information longer, and practice the skills needed to write a research paper. In addition to these benefits, writing a summary is great training for the reading sections of state tests and for the SAT and ACT. The skills needed to write a summary will help when looking for main ideas, and every reading test includes questions about the main ideas. While there are many opinions about what makes a good summary, most people agree on the following characteristics:
	▶ Summaries are significantly shorter than the original
	▶ Summaries follow the organizational pattern of the original
	▶ Summaries include the main ideas
	▶ Summaries do not include the opinion of the person who wrote the summary
	▶ Summaries paraphrase the original author's words
	This assignment is a specific type of a summary, called a ten percent summary; that is, a summary of an article that is only ten percent of the original length. A ten percent summary is best used to condense nonfiction or expository writing that is between 500 and 2,000 words long, the length of most passages on reading tests and many magazine or newspaper articles.
Writer's Purpose	You will write the main ideas in your own words. Include the most important details if the word limit permits. You will want clear and accurate information with no opinion. Remember, this is a summary—not an evaluation.
Writer's Role	You will take the role of a researcher or analyst who has been hired by MainIdeas.com to distill information for interested adults.
Audience	Your audience will be busy, smart adults who want to get the main ideas of articles to see if they should read the article completely.
Form	You will write a summary of your assigned article in approximately ten percent of the words—not exactly ten percent, but approximately ten percent. For example, if you have a 1,000 word article, you would write a 90 to 110 word summary; if 1,250 words, write 110 to 140 words.

Focus Correction Areas	1. Include <u>S.</u> A."T". (source underlined, author, title appears in quotes) in the summary _____ points
	2. Include _____ to _____ main points in approximately ten percent of the words _____ points
	3. To be determined _____ points

Procedure	Before writing your summary, you will complete several activities.
	☐ Read the article once through quickly, then take care to read the first few paragraphs (10 to 20 percent of the article) carefully. The first few paragraphs usually contain the author's position on the topic. Read the first sentence of the middle paragraphs (middle 60 to 80 percent of the article) carefully. They usually tell the main ideas. Read the last paragraphs (last 10 to 20 percent of the article) carefully. They usually sum up the main points.
	☐ Draft your summary. You may want to keep a running word count by occasionally noting how many words you have written over the end marks of your sentences. With this technique, you always know about how close you are to your word count goal of ten percent of the words.
	☐ Read your summary in a one-foot voice; make any changes that you believe will improve your draft.
	☐ Work with a partner to peer edit your paragraph and get feedback.
	☐ Rewrite your second draft with all your improvements.
	☐ Due date _____.

Samples of "to be determined" FCAs	▶ Correctly include a specific number of technical words from the article. For example, use 5 of the 10 words highlighted by the teacher.
	▶ Include one short, correctly punctuated quotation (3 to 6 words) in your summary.
	▶ No more than 4 words in a row taken from the original text.
	▶ Conventions (for example: spelling, complete sentences, capitalization, correct use of commas, legible handwriting).

Vocabulary Cards: Using Cards to Master Technical Vocabulary

Project Summary

To demonstrate knowledge in a field, one must be able to use the vocabulary of that field, but your textbook introduces vocabulary a little at a time and then doesn't review it. Consequently, you may learn the vocabulary for the chapter test and never study it again! To learn and really remember, it is more effective to study frequently in short bursts than to study just once for a long time. When it comes to learning vocabulary, one of the easiest and most efficient ways is with vocabulary cards. This assignment requires that you create your own set of vocabulary cards. In fact, just creating the cards will help you begin to remember the words. Do your best. We will be repeating this assignment frequently during the year. You'll end up with an impressive collection of vocabulary cards. Also, I'll be testing on vocabulary all year long, and I will include words from the full year, not just the last unit—so don't lose your cards.

Writer's Purpose

You will create clear information, with accurate definitions of important concepts or words. In addition, you will write a sentence using each vocabulary word that will help you remember the word and its meaning.

Writer's Role

You will be writing as yourself, a concerned student who sees this assignment as a relatively easy way to get a good grade and produce something that will help you learn. (It is interesting to note that there are companies that hire writers to produce vocabulary cards; for example, the Princeton Review has tear-out vocabulary cards in the back of its College Board prep books, and Spark Notes produces boxed sets of vocabulary cards in a wide range of subjects.)

Audience

You will be creating these cards primarily for your own use, but you may find that it is helpful to study cards created by other students.

Form

Print the word on one side and, if possible, an illustration that helps you remember the word. Side two has the part of speech (noun, verb, etc.) and meaning or meanings of the word. Side two should also have an original sentence that helps convey the meaning of the word through the context. See example cards for more detail.

Focus Correction Areas

1. _____ cards with word and complete definition (part of speech and meaning or meanings) _____ points

2. Complete sentence that conveys meaning of the word _____ points

3. Graphic illustration _____ points

Procedure

- ☐ Before writing your vocabulary cards, you will complete several activities.
- ☐ Using a Type One writing assignment, generate a list of all possible relevant vocabulary words for the current topic.
- ☐ Using the list generated in the above step, create a final list of important or critical words for the cards, while eliminating any obscure or obvious vocabulary words.
- ☐ Create first draft of cards, due on _____.
- ☐ Share your cards with a partner to make sure they are accurate and fulfill the requirements set by the FCAs.
- ☐ Final draft of cards with all improvements due on _____.

FOCUS SHEET — Sample Vocabulary Cards

Side One	Side Two
Word: Alopecia Illustration:	Definition: Noun—loss of hair, baldness Sentence: To cure alopecia, people will spend money on hair plugs, wigs, medicine, and vitamins.
Word: Dice Illustration:	Definition: Verb—to cut into small pieces of about the same size. Sentence: We had to dice the carrots again because we cut them unevenly.
Word: Jargon Illustration:	Definition: Noun—specialized vocabulary of a trade or group. Also, words difficult to understand. Sentence: Now that I've studied medical technology for two years, I know so much medical jargon I sound like a doctor, or should I say physician.

Side One

Word: _____

Illustration:

Side One

Word: _____

Illustration:

Side One

Word: _____

Illustration:

Side One

Word: _____

Illustration:

Side One

Word: _____

Illustration:

Side One

Word: _____

Illustration:

Side One

Word: _____

Illustration:

Side One

Word: _____

Illustration:

Definition:

Sentence:

✂ -

Definition:

Sentence:

✂ -

Definition:

Sentence:

✂ -

Definition:

Sentence:

Definition:

Sentence:

Definition:

Sentence:

Definition:

Sentence:

Definition:

Sentence:

Similar, but Different: Comparing and Contrasting When the Differences Are Subtle

Project Summary	Being able to identify the differences between two things that are similar requires careful observation, insight, and precise thinking. Learning this process of comparison and contrast is not only a skill you will use during your education but throughout your life—when you select a college, buy a car, choose a job or career, or vote for a candidate. In this project, you will be writing for a student who will be taking this course next year and who values your advice on how to make the distinctions you are making.
Writer's Purpose	Your purpose is to be analytical, identifying and clarifying similarities and differences.
Writer's Role	You are writing as a student who "knows the ropes" in this course and can pass on helpful information to a future student.
Audience	Your audience is a future student who will appreciate your help in making the distinctions you are making in this piece of writing. Your choice of language for this project should be precise and reflect your knowledge of the topic.
Form	Your explanation will be a multi-paragraph analysis.
Focus Correction Areas	1. At least _____ similarities between the two _____ points 2. At least _____ distinctions between the two _____ points 3. To be determined _____ points
Procedure	Before writing your analysis, you will complete several activities. ❑ Type One writing: Write down why you think _____ and _____ might be confused in the minds of a less-experienced student. Why would someone confuse the two? ❑ Gather information or make notes on what you are going to compare. ❑ Use the Focus Sheet for Comparing and Contrasting to determine the similarities and differences. Summarize the similarities and differences that are in the Venn diagram at the bottom of the Focus Sheet. ❑ Draft your explanation. Due on _____.

❑ Read your paper in a one-foot voice; make any changes you feel will improve your explanation.

❑ Work with a partner and get feedback on your analysis; double-check your FCAs to make sure you have done a good job in those areas.

❑ Write a second draft with all your improvements.

❑ Due date _____.

FOCUS SHEET Comparing and Contrasting Venn Diagram

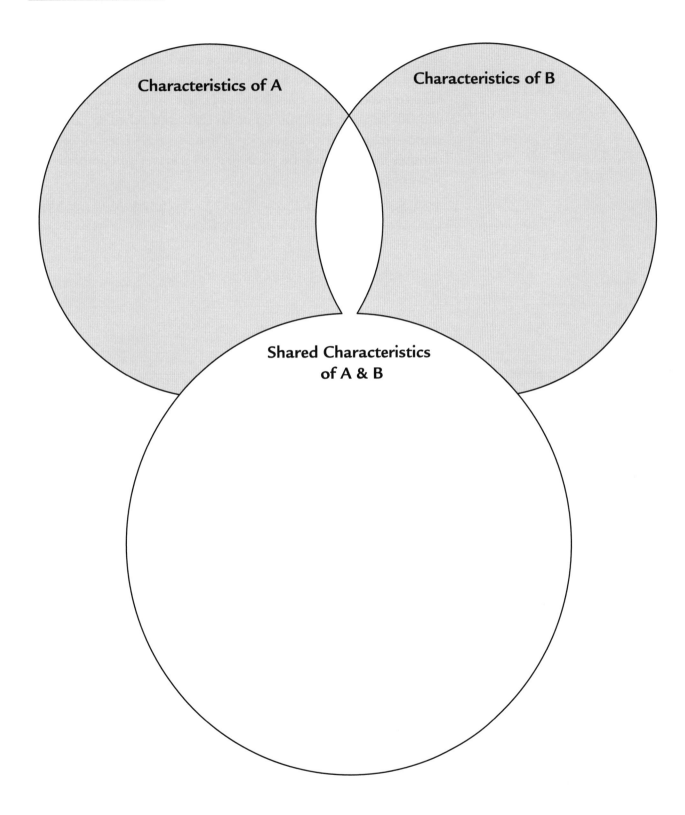

Characteristics of A

Characteristics of B

Shared Characteristics
of A & B

The Short Persuasive Essay: Taking a Stand on an Issue

Project Summary	Students who take the SAT or ACT are often required to take a stand on an issue or agree or disagree with a quote. Even if you will never take these national college admissions exams, you will be confronted over time with opinions of others and will have to make a clear case for your beliefs. In this assignment you will be given a quotation or an issue and asked to take a stand—to agree or disagree. Since the actual SAT test is 25 minutes long, you will be given just 25 minutes to complete this assignment. *(Teacher will insert relevant quotation or issue in the space below.)*
Writer's Purpose	Your purpose is to take a clear stand (or position) and defend your opinion in a persuasive way.
Writer's Role	You will write as yourself, a student with an opinion.
Audience	Your audience will be your teacher and classmates. You could also imagine readers from across the country who do not know you and have been hired to read and score your essay.
Form	You will write a multi-paragraph essay in 25 minutes.
Focus Correction Areas	1. Clear statement of opinion _____ points 2. Two to three compelling reasons with supporting details (one or two reasons must be academic) _____ points 3. To be determined _____ points

Procedure

Before writing your assignment, you will complete several activities in class:

☐ Fill in the Short Persuasive Essay Focus Sheet.

☐ Draft your essay.

☐ Read your draft in a one-foot voice; make any necessary changes to improve your essay.

Optional Steps:

☐ Work with a partner to peer edit and get feedback; double-check your FCAs to be sure you have completed the assignment.

☐ Rewrite your second draft with all your improvements.

☐ Due date _____.

Samples of "to be determined" FCAs

▶ Strong conclusion

▶ Four part thesis statement

▶ Sentence variety

▶ Use one **?** or **!** sentence

▶ A short, catchy title

▶ An opposing position/refuted

▶ Clear organization (paragraphs and/or transitions)

▶ Two or more vivid verbs, circled

▶ Avoid the generic "you"

▶ Avoid colloquial language

▶ Use specific detailed examples—avoid the hypothetical

▶ Complete sentences

▶ Correct spelling—especially of common words (your, you're)

Notes on the Short Persuasive Essay Focus Sheet

The short persuasive essay, usually about 30 minutes, has become the standard for many writing tests. Some states require a persuasive essay in the third and fourth grades, and these essays continue on to the SAT and ACT for college admissions and are used in the adult world in job applications. Being a good persuasive writer is a skill you can use for the rest of your life.

Persuasive essay questions or prompts can usually be grouped into one of two kinds. One kind of prompt asks a question and then asks the writer to create an answer and argue why the answer is a good one. An example of this kind of prompt is this eighth grade question from Oklahoma:

> If you could live during a different period in history, what period would you choose? Why would you make that choice? Support your ideas with details.

The hardest part in this type of prompt is to remember to brainstorm choices before you begin to write so that you have a choice you can defend with reasons and details. Also, if you have time, you can explain why you rejected one of the choices from your list.

The second kind of prompt, one you would see on the SAT or ACT, requires you to agree or disagree with a position. Here is an example from the ACT:

> Many high school libraries use some of their limited funding to subscribe to popular magazines with articles that are interesting to students. Despite limited funding, some educators support this practice because they think having these magazines available encourages students to read. Other educators think school libraries should not use limited funds to subscribe to these magazines because they may not be related to academic subjects. In your opinion, should high school libraries use some of their limited funding to subscribe to popular magazines? In your essay, take a position on this question. You may write about either one of the two points of view given, or you may present a different point of view on this question. Use specific reasons and examples to support your position.

The Short Persuasive Essay Focus Sheet is helpful for both kinds of persuasive essays but may be most helpful with the agree/disagree kind by providing an outline of reasons for and against almost any topic. It then provides a quick, effective way of turning the reasons into a clear thesis statement. Be patient. The first few times you use the focus sheet may be time consuming, but as you practice using it, you will become quicker and your plan for your essay will come together faster, leaving more time to focus on your writing skills. Remember, the persuasive essay is a writing test. There is no right or wrong answer. The test scorers want to see how you develop your ideas in writing, not if you found the "right" answer.

FOCUS SHEET Short Persuasive Essay Sheet—
HELPS: Getting and Organizing Your Ideas

REASONS FOR	REASONS AGAINST
H Historic, Political, Legal	**H** Historic, Political, Legal
E Economic, Resource Utilization	**E** Economic, Resource Utilization
L Literary, Aesthetic	**L** Literary, Aesthetic
P Personal, Ethical, Religious	**P** Personal, Ethical, Religious
S Scientific	**S** Scientific

Position → Yes
→ Under certain conditions/circumstances
→ No

Reason 1 _____
Reason 2 _____
Reason 3 _____

THESIS STATEMENT: Topic / Position / 2 to 3 Reasons without "I."

_____

_____

4

Highly Recommended Assignments

The last chapter described four essential assignments. This chapter will describe seven additional high impact assignments that can be used in any subject, grades four to twelve, with only minor modifications based on students' reading levels and writing experience. The four essential assignments have meta-analytical research to support their value, these six highly recommended assignments meet two other, equally important criteria.

The first criterion is both students and teachers enjoy writing and reading them. All involve, in one way or another, students reflecting on what is happening in class in a thoughtful yet critical way. For example, selecting test questions, identifying strengths and weaknesses, and making recommendations are all wonderful assignments that show respect for students' opinions yet demand thoughtful answers.

The second criterion is that they provide the teacher with organized, structured feedback that can be reviewed and processed to plan for future classes. Some of the most significant changes I have made in my own teaching have come as a result of reading students' responses to these assignments. Our students do not have much real-world experience or expertise, but the one thing they are close to being experts at is school. These assignments acknowledge their experience and ask students to think critically about it. The following pages provide a brief description of each of the assignments with a page reference where the actual seven element assignment can be found.

1. Writing a "Who Am I?" autobiographical sketch about a classmate

Interviewing and writing about a classmate

The "Who Am I" autobiography on page 88 is one of my two or three personal favorite writing assignments. To this day, I always include it on the first day of my three to five day courses for the same reasons I recommend it to teachers: it provides personal information about my students that I can use to build relationships, it begins to create community and a spirit of collaboration, it provides a fun, easy-to-do writing assessment, it tends to produce high grades, it starts the class on a positive note, and—if taken to a Type Four or Type Five—it provides an early experience with most aspects of the Collins Writing Program.

2. Class Log

Creating a description of class for a student who was absent

The "Class Log" on page 92 requires two students to summarize each class. It is a little different from the other assignments because only two students per day are required to complete a class log rather than the whole class. I have designed it this way to give the teacher a chance to have a course documented but not to have to read numerous class logs each day. But for the first week or two, everyone in class might be required to complete a log to make sure the assignment is clear. During this introductory period, some of the best logs should be read out loud to the class to establish high expectations.

3. Create a Test

Creating a possible test for the unit the class has just studied

The "Create a Test" assignment on page 95 asks students to develop an end-of-unit or end-of-chapter test. Beyond the obvious benefit of saving the teacher time and effort in test construction, this assignment involves the student directly in developing a fair test, writing for an audience in addition to the teacher (their classmates), and writing for a real purpose. In addition, the oral reading and sharing phase create excellent review and study activities. Also, the actual tests provide an opportunity to see if the students have developed an understanding of the important facts and questions that make up the unit. These student-made tests can help the teacher discover what students feel they should know—always an important insight—and they provide almost an unlimited source of practice tests, real tests, and make-up tests.

4. Study Guide

Predicting essay questions, explaining why your predicted questions should be on a test, and answering the questions

The "Study Guide" on page 97 is a variation of the "Create a Test," but it requires students to explain *why* they created their suggested essay questions and to fully answer each essay; whereas the "Create a Test" only requires the students to write essay questions but not to answer them. The "Create a Test" and "Study Guide" assignments can be used interchangeably.

5. End of Unit Reflection

Writing a letter to a future student describing how to do well in class

The "End of Unit Reflection" on page 99 is designed to help students think about how they have done on a past unit and share their knowledge with a student who will be in the same class next year. By creating an audience, next year's student, I have found that some of my students were remarkably candid in their assessment of their own work habits and, upon reflection of what they had written, became more able to motivate themselves to do better in the future. This assignment has also been very helpful to me because students will tell "next year's student" about my expectations—even the ones that I was unaware of myself. Additionally, the compositions provide a valuable insight into students' study and work habits. When students with poor study habits hear about the study habits of students they think are naturally smart, they sometimes discover new study techniques: for example, reviewing material for a half-hour each day for three days before a test rather than cramming for an hour and a half the night   before. At its best, the End of Unit Reflection assignment can be an exercise in positive peer pressure and can help teachers discover the unclear or mixed messages they may have sent during a unit.

6. It's a Must!

Making thoughtful recommendations

The "It's a Must! Making Thoughtful Recommendations" assignment on page 100 is similar to "End of Unit Reflection" but asks students to reflect on the course itself rather than their own work in the course. This assignment asks students to do what they do most naturally—judge a course, but to do so in a "respectful and well thought out" way. The assignment is written to try to avoid personal criticism of the teacher, and I would consider the maturity of my class before giving it out, but if writers should write about what they know, then this assignment is on target and should produce helpful feedback.

7. Letter to Next Year's Teacher (and possibly others)

Reflecting on what you have learned

While I love to begin my classes with the "Who Am I" autobiography, I love to end them with the "Letter to Next Year's Teacher" on page 102. Assignments that require a student to analyze his or her own learning are becoming more and more common in all areas of the curriculum. School districts that have adopted a portfolio system require a piece similar to this letter to serve as an introduction to the portfolio, informing the reader about the contents and providing an analysis of the author's learning. Some states are considering a state writing test that would require the student to write about his or her strengths and weaknesses as a writer.

This letter can be written in multiple drafts, leading to a Type Five final product. Each draft could have its own set of focus correction areas and each would receive credit. The first draft might contain only content focus correction areas listed in the assignment (summary of year, strengths and weaknesses, and favorite assignment); the second draft, style focus correction areas (sentence variety, transitions, and strong verbs); and the third draft, mechanics (spelling, punctuation, and neatness or penmanship). Or, these three sets of focus correction areas might be combined to create a review of all the FCAs covered in the past year.

Whether the assignment is a basic Type Three or Type Four, or if the assignment goes through multiple drafts with many focus correction areas and many audiences, I believe the "Letter to Next Year's Teacher" provides the best feedback a teacher can receive on the effectiveness of his or her program.

Writing a "Who Am I?" Autobiographical Sketch about a Classmate

Interviewing a Classmate and Using the Information for an Autobiographical Sketch

Project Summary	This assignment will help you practice three essential skills: listening, speaking and writing. These are important skills for this class—and for life. In this project, you will use all these skills as you get to know some of your new classmates. Over the next several days, you will have time to interview three different classmates. Then I am going to ask you to use your notes to write a "Who Am I?" autobiography about one of the classmates you interviewed. You will write the sketch as though you are that classmate and include information that would allow others to guess who "you" are.
Writer's Purpose	Your purpose is to be informative. Your goal is to tell enough about the person you interviewed to enable classmates to guess that person's identity. Feel free to be entertaining, but do not embarrass the classmate you are describing. No cheap shots!
Writer's Role	After gathering information about your classmate, you will write a "Who Am I?" autobiography in the first person (use I) as though you were that person.
Audience	You are writing for your classmates who may not know a great deal about "you." Based on the information you provide, they will be trying to guess who "you" are.
Form	This will be an autobiographical sketch (15-25 lines) about "you."
Focus Correction Areas	1. Accurate information—eight to ten facts (use information from your questionnaire, but do not use any physical characteristics) _____ points 2. Write in first person (use I, never he or she) _____ points 3. To be determined _____ points
Procedure	Before writing your autobiographical sketch, you will complete several activities. ☐ Type One writing: In six lines or more, describe the kind of information you think should be included in an autobiography

to make it informative and interesting. We will discuss your responses in class.

☐ We will review the suggested questions on the Interviewer's Notebook Focus Sheet. You may add other questions of your own.

☐ During three different class meetings, you will spend part of each period interviewing a different classmate (and being interviewed by that classmate). Take notes and label them.

☐ On the fourth day, I will announce which of the three interviews I want you to turn into the "Who am I?" autobiography.

☐ Draft your autobiographical sketch. Due date: _____.

☐ Read your draft in a one-foot voice; make changes you feel will improve your piece.

☐ Work with a partner to get feedback on your autobiographical sketch; double-check your FCAs to make sure you have done a good job in those areas.

☐ Write a second draft with all of your improvements.

☐ Due date: _____.

Interviewer's Notebook

Questions About Family

Do you have brothers or sisters? Names? Ages?

_____

_____

_____

What is one interesting fact about a member of your family?

_____

_____

_____

Have you ever lived in another community? How does it compare to this one?

_____

_____

_____

Does your family have any special customs or traditions?

_____

_____

_____

Questions About Interests

What are your favorite or least favorite...

Foods

_____

_____

Books, TV shows, movies or videos

_____

_____

Hobbies

_____

_____

Class in school

_____

_____

Ways to kill time

_____

_____

Questions About the Past and Future

If you could live anywhere in the world, where would it be? Why?

_____

_____

_____

What career or job goals do you have? College plans?

_____

_____

_____

What would be the perfect age? Why?

_____

_____

_____

What awards or special recognition have you earned?

_____

_____

_____

What do you think your friends would say are your best attributes?

_____

_____

_____

What was your proudest moment?

_____

_____

_____

Do you have any suggestions to the teacher that would help make
this class the best possible experience?

_____

_____

_____

Other Questions

_____

_____

_____

_____

_____

_____

Class Log

Creating a Description of Class for a Student Who Was Absent

Project Summary

This year our class will keep a class log—a day-by-day description of what went on in each class. The log by itself is a three-ring binder with two sections: the back section has blank class log worksheets, the front section is for completed class logs. Each day two members of this class are responsible for filling out class log sheets and inserting them in the log. As a result of this assignment, we will have an accurate record of our class meetings that will be especially helpful for students who are absent or who have missed class. It will also help me make sure I do what I said I would do when I said it. By having two students complete the assignment each day, we will have a way of cross-checking for accurate information.

Writer's Purpose

This assignment is both informative and practical: writing in which the main intent is to provide clear information.

Writer's Role

You will be writing as yourself.

Audience

The students of this class, especially students who missed class; therefore, try to be as complete and clear as you can.

Form

Fill out the class log worksheet page provided in the class log. The completed worksheet is due at the beginning of class the next school day. The worksheet may be handwritten or typed, but it must be easy to read.

Focus Correction Areas

1. Each section must be answered accurately. If there is nothing to write in a section, indicate that; do not leave a section blank _____ points

2. Attach any handouts and announcements to your class log worksheet _____ points

3. To be determined _____ points

Procedure

☐ Make sure you know which day you have responsibility for the log. Since two students per day fill out the log, it should be easy to determine how frequently your turn will come up.

☐ Take careful notes in class. If you want, you may take two worksheets, one to fill out in class and one to recopy for the final copy.

☐ If you have any questions about the accuracy of your information, check with your classmates, but do not check your log with the one other classmate assigned to complete the log on your day—do them independently!

☐ When you have finished, read it out loud, check it for the FCAs and do not forget to sign, date, and put it in the log book. If you forget to put it in the book on time, you will not receive credit for the assignment.

Class Log Worksheet

FCA _____ points _____ Completed by _____

(Signature)

FCA _____ points _____

FCA _____ points _____   Date _____

1. Summary of class (what topics were covered, important examples or questions, notes from the board, pages in text. Attach copy of handouts, worksheets, etc.):

_____

_____

_____

_____

_____

_____

_____

_____

_____

_____

_____

_____

_____

_____

_____

_____

_____

_____

_____

2. Announcements:

_____

_____

_____

_____

_____

3. Assignment(s) (due dates):

_____

_____

_____

_____

_____

_____

Create a Test

Creating a Possible Test for the Unit the Class Has Just Studied

Project Summary

Now that we are close to the end of this unit, it is time to think about a test. This assignment requires you to create a test for this class.

Tests often have two types of questions: objective and essays. Examples of objective test questions are multiple choice, true/false, and fill-ins. Objective questions require specific information. Essay questions, especially well-written essay questions, do not test specific facts as much as they test ability to analyze, explain, or argue. This assignment requires you to create ten objective questions (multiple choice, fill-in, or true/false) and two essay questions.

Writer's Purpose

This writing assignment requires practical/informative writing skills; that is, all the questions should be clear and easy to understand.

Writer's Role

You will be writing as if you were the teacher. Your goal is to create a fair test that questions students on the most important elements in the unit.

Audience

The students in this class. If I receive a test that I believe is well done, the creator will not only get an A for this assignment, but will also have the benefit of taking the test he/she created.

Form

You will create ten objective questions. For each objective question, include the correct answer in the margin beside each question. Additionally, you will write two essay questions with two or three FCAs each. You do not have to answer the essays.

Remember, a good essay question does not need to be extremely difficult, but it should require the person answering it to think and analyze, not just remember facts. When designing the test, assume students will have about 10 minutes for each essay and about 10 to 15 minutes for the objective section. The total test should take about 35–40 minutes.

Focus Correction Areas

1. Ten clearly written, objective questions with answers in margin _____ points

2. Two essay questions with 2–3 FCAs each _____ points

3. Complete sentences and correct spelling of all words. (Watch for question marks at the end of your questions.) _____ points

Procedure

☐ Review all materials, notes, etc., you have on this unit. Determine what is most important.

☐ Create your questions, both objective and essay, with FCAs, due in class on _____ .

☐ In class on _____ we will turn your test from Type Three writing to Type Four through oral reading and peer editing.

☐ Your final draft—Type Four—of the test is due in class on _____ .

Study Guide

Predicting, Explaining, and Answering Essay Questions

Project Summary	Many times the hardest part of preparing for a test is determining what is important to study and what is not. This assignment asks you to create a study guide for the unit we have just finished by creating two essay questions, explaining why these questions are important, and then writing answers to the questions.
Writer's Purpose	This assignment requires practical/informative writing; its main intent is to provide clear, accurate information organized as correct answers to potential essay test questions. Feel free to use your notes and any other relevant sources.
Writer's Role	You will be writing as yourself. Any insight you can bring to help another student prepare for the unit test will be appreciated.
Audience	Imagine you are writing to a classmate who has missed a substantial number of classes. The student needs your help to determine which questions are most likely to appear on the test and the answers to these questions.
Form	Your study guide should take the form of two, three-part essays. In each part you should state one essay question, explain why it is an important question, and then correctly answer the question. Your sentences should be clear, and your paragraphs well organized and easy to read. The final product should be _____ to _____ handwritten lines long.
Focus Correction Areas	1. List two important essay questions with focus correction areas and explain to your reader why you picked each of these questions _____ points
	2. Correctly answer the two essay questions you created _____ points
	3. To be determined _____ points
Procedure	☐ Read and review your textbook and any other resources on the unit.
	☐ Try to anticipate any questions that might be asked on the unit test.

❑ Make a list of at least seven questions and then select the best two.

❑ Check to see if the information you have answers the questions you selected. Get help if you need additional information.

❑ Discuss your questions and the information you have with a classmate.

❑ Draft your study guide. List each question, then the reason why the question is important and likely to be asked on a test and, finally, answer each question. Due date _____.

❑ Read your draft out loud. See if it is easy to read and check for the FCAs.

❑ When you are confident the draft is accurate and well done, have another student read it to you out loud and listen for problems in the FCAs.

❑ Make any necessary revisions or edits and recopy.

❑ Final study guide due date _____.

End of Unit Reflection

Writing a Letter to a Future Student Describing How to Do Well in Class

Project Summary	Now that we have completed a major unit, I would like you to reflect on how you did. To do this, I am asking you to write a letter to a student who will be taking this course next year. Assume this student is very much like yourself (same or similar work habits, interests, etc.). Tell this student how you did and give advice on how to do well on this unit next year.
Writer's Purpose	This assignment is part analytical/expository and part practical/informative. In the first part of your letter you must analyze how you did in this unit and why. In the second part you must give clear information to next year's student about what to do to be successful.
Writer's Role	You will be writing as yourself.
Audience	A student, one year from now, who is about to begin the unit we just finished. Assume this student is similar to you—has your work habits, academic strengths and weaknesses, and your out-of-class responsibilities.
Form	An informal, Type Three friendly letter, addressed to next year's student. Don't worry about addresses, etc., just title it "Letter to Next Year's Student" on the fifth line down.
Focus Correction Areas	1. Analyze how you did and why _____ points 2. Give three specific suggestions to next year's student on how to do well on the unit we have just completed _____ points 3. To be determined _____ points
Procedure	☐ Think about your grades for this unit and review your study habits, class performance, homework, etc., during this unit. List things you did well and what you could have improved. ☐ List some recommendations or suggestions for next year's student. ☐ Write up your ideas from the first two steps into a letter due on _____. ☐ In class on _____, we will improve these letters through oral reading and revising.

It's a Must! Making Thoughtful Recommendations

Convincing Your Teacher About the Importance of Certain Aspects of This Class

Project Summary	Making well-considered recommendations is something we do throughout our lives. In this writing assignment, you will make recommendations to me that will influence the way I teach this course in the future. My problem is that there is always more content to teach in this course than there is time to teach it. My goal is to spend more time on fewer, critical aspects of our subject. Some of the ideas, concepts, and skills we have spent time on cannot be eliminated because they are critical to the course or prerequisites for other things we do in this class. Which units, chapters, readings, or projects have we completed that you feel are essential for this course and deserve even more time? If we are to spend more time on those areas, then something must be eliminated or de-emphasized. Which aspects of this class do you feel are not essential? I need your recommendations as I make plans for teaching this course next year. You will put your recommendations to me in the form of a letter.
Writer's Purpose	Your purpose is to be persuasive, so be sure that your recommendations are supported with solid reasons and examples.
Writer's Role	You will write as yourself, an experienced student who has a good understanding of what is and what is not critical to this course.
Audience	You are writing to me, your teacher. I am open to your ideas or I would not be giving this assignment, but I also will be more easily convinced if your tone is respectful and well thought out.
Form	You will write a multi-paragraph letter.
Focus Correction Areas	1. Two or three "Musts" (describe two or three aspects of this class you feel are essential; for each, give several specific reasons why they must be kept) _____ points 2. Two "Cuts" (describe two aspects of this class that you feel could be eliminated or given less emphasis; for each, give specific reasons) _____ points 3. To be determined _____ points

Procedure

Before writing your letter, you will complete several activities.

☐ Type One writing: Write eight lines or more about the essential skills or concepts that an incoming student must master in order to succeed in this class or lab.

☐ As a class, we will discuss how we have allocated our time this year by reviewing major projects, units of study, and other activities, and approximately how much time we have devoted to each.

☐ After this discussion, decide which are essential and which are nonessential aspects of this class. Draft your letter. Due on: _____.

☐ Read your draft in a one-foot voice; make any changes you feel will improve your letter.

☐ Work with a partner to get feedback on your letter; double-check your FCAs to make sure you have done a good job in those areas.

☐ Write a second draft with all of your improvements.

☐ Due date: _____.

Letter to Next Year's Teacher (and possibly others)

Reflecting on What You Have Learned

Project Summary	There was a famous teacher at Columbia University, John Dewey, whom people credit with the phrase, "Learn by doing," but that is not what he said. What he said was that you learn by reflecting on what you have done. This assignment will give you a chance to do exactly that. You will write a letter to next year's teacher describing what you did this year, how you feel you did overall, and what assignment you liked the most.

When you have successfully completed the assignment, you will have had a chance to "reflect on what you've done," and your next teacher will get an insight into your strengths and weaknesses and will, therefore, be better able to teach you. |
Writer's Purpose	This assignment is both informative and analytical. Give details about what you have learned, analyze your strengths and weaknesses, and describe your favorite assignment.
Writer's Role	You will be writing as yourself, trying to be honest and clear, and ultimately making a good first impression on next year's teacher. Use this chance to show how insightful you are about yourself.
Audience	Most teachers who give this assignment send it to next year's teacher. Some send a copy home to parents or guardians, and some teachers even make copies for student files for counselors.
Form	You will be given more details about how formal or informal this letter should be, but the letter should be at least five paragraphs. Include an introduction about yourself, at least three detailed paragraphs about each of the FCAs, and a concluding paragraph.
Focus Correction Areas	1. A descriptive summary of this year's program, including information about the numbers and types of assignments completed, the focus correction areas covered, procedures used in class, and any other information that would provide a detailed picture of the class _____ points

2. A description of your strengths and weaknesses with supporting examples and details taken from your own writing _____ points |

3. A description of your favorite assignment or project completed during the year with supporting reasons and details _____ points

Procedure

Before writing your letter, you will complete several activities:

☐ In a series of Type One writing activities, you will make a list of the subject, units, topics, and assignments you have completed.

☐ You will share these lists to make sure they are complete.

☐ You will then place your list in chronological order.

☐ You will also list and group your strengths and weaknesses as a student in this class.

☐ Next, you will think about all your assignments and select the one that was your favorite. Give reasons and details to support your selection.

☐ You will then draft the three main parts of the letter (describe year, describe strengths and weaknesses, and favorite assignment). Be sure to include details and personal opinions.

☐ Once the three main parts of the letter are complete, you will write a one paragraph introduction with some personal information. You can include information about your family, goals, achievements, favorite subjects, how you like to learn, etc.

☐ To finish your draft, you will write a concluding paragraph summing up your first four paragraphs and ending on a positive note.

☐ Read your draft letter in a one-foot voice; make any changes that you believe will improve your draft.

☐ Work with a partner to peer edit the FCAs and get feedback.

☐ Rewrite your second draft with all your improvements.

☐ Due date _____.

CHAPTER 5

Classroom Snapshots:
Adapting the Collins Writing Program to Your Students

One of the most helpful theories I have ever learned was situational leadership developed by Paul Hersey and Ken Blanchard. They suggest that a leader (in our case, a teacher) must consider the maturity of the group to be effective. They define maturity as having three components.

▶ Experience with the task

▶ Willingness to take responsibility

▶ Achievement motivation

In schools, the teacher would think about the class and try to determine a general level of maturity considering the three components. Of course, this is not an easy diagnosis to make because all classes have a wide range; nevertheless, many classes have personalities and that is what we are diagnosing, the general maturity of the class.

Once the diagnosis is made, the teacher has two variables to adjust: task orientation (concern for the job) and relationship (concern for the students). The less mature the students are, the more task oriented the teacher becomes. As the students become more mature, the teacher adds relationship. This does not mean that the teacher is uncaring; it simply means there is a strong emphasis on getting the job done. For example, if a group of students were very immature (no real experience doing the task, no real desire to do well, and unable to take responsibility on their own), the teacher would focus, in our case, on the writing assignment and be all business: strict, clear, with deadlines. Hersey and Blanchard described this style as **telling**. As the students have more experience with the writing task, act more responsibly, and want to achieve, the teacher adds more relationship (described as **selling**). As the students get even more mature because of their extensive experience and, let's hope, success, the teacher emphasizes the relationship component (described as **participating**). Finally, in the class we all dream of, the students are experienced, responsible, and desire to achieve at a high level. In this class, the teacher backs away from both the task and relationship and lets the students help decide what assignments need to be done (described as **delegating**). The pyramid on page 108 summarizes how this theory may be used with the Collins Writing Program, but a few illustrations or snapshots may help clarify the relationship even more.

▶ Snapshot One

First, let's imagine a middle school science class that could be considered immature. They do not seem to want to learn science, don't appear to take notes or do homework, and they play with the lab equipment. In this type of class, the teacher would create a highly structured environment with many Type One and Type Two assignments to build success. These assignments would probably start out relatively easy and would be given on a regular basis. The teacher would then move to short, probably paragraph length, Type Three assignments using the information tested in Type Two. For example, the teacher may give the class the Venn diagram from the comparing and contrasting assignment and ask them to fill in a specified number of ways plant and animal cells are different and alike. If the students were successful at this activity, they would have to write a Type Three paragraph comparing and contrasting plant and animal cells. If this assignment is successful, the students could be encouraged to peer edit these comparison and contrast essays (Type Four). Eventually, the class would be doing vocabulary cards and summaries and more elaborated comparisons and contrasts during the year. There would probably be no Type Fives and only a few highly elaborated assignments because the maturity of the students is not at a point where longer assignments would be successful. That would come next year, building on the success of this year.

▶ Snapshot Two

Now, let us imagine a class of high school students who are neither mature nor immature, middle-of-road kids. The teacher may start with frequent Type Ones and Type Twos, and because the students react positively to the structure and, we hope, have success, could quickly move to some of the essential writing assignments (vocabulary cards, summaries, etc.). Because of the structure (task) the students continue to do well, so the teacher designs some seven element,

Type Four assignments that fit into the curriculum perfectly and have varied audiences, roles, and forms that the students enjoy writing. Eventually, the teacher has the students edit some of these assignments, turning them into Type Five assignments to be displayed publicly. During the course of the year, the frequency of the Type Ones and Type Twos diminishes, but does not stop, while the frequency and complexity of the Type Threes and Type Fours increases, and the students, with practice, become conscientious peer editors. They started further along and end further along.

▶ Snapshot Three

Finally, let us imagine a dream class. They love the subject (had terrific past teachers), want to do very well, and know what it takes to be successful. This class still gets Type One and Type Two assignments, not so much to encourage regular study but so that the teacher can check on understanding of complex concepts and communicate to the students what type of questions are important. This dream class may or may not need some of the essential assignments because they already know how to summarize, compare and contrast, and write short persuasive essays. Rather, this teacher would create custom-made seven element assignments, encourage peer editing, and eventually have the students help design the assignments themselves. These are students who would volunteer to do some of the highly recommended assignments in Chapter Four, such as the Class Log because of its innate value, and take the End of Unit Reflection and Study Guide assignments very seriously. In this type of class the FCAs would be more broad, covering a wide range of skills; for example, the multi-paragraph essay form and reasons with support may be assumed but compelling reasons, succinctly developed may be very appropriate, as would a strong metaphor or vivid verbs. This is a class where there would be frequent Type Fives that would not be too difficult for the teacher to evaluate because the students have the maturity (experience, responsibility, and motivation) to do the job well before the teacher reviews it and well done papers are easy to grade.

I have been in some communities where classes of high school juniors and seniors were very immature writers. Writing tasks needed to be broken down into relatively discreet parts and only frequent quizzes (Type Two) kept the students studying and note-taking. These were classes who needed direct, repeated instruction on, for example, how to summarize a nonfiction article and immediate, specific feedback (FCAs) on how they were doing to keep them focused. The focus correction areas were stated very clearly and there needed to be frequent modeling on the overhead to explain exactly what the teacher was looking for. Peer editing was eventually successful, but the teacher had to be watchful and structured to make it productive.

On the other hand, I have also been in other communities where the fourth graders were very mature writers. There were fewer Type One and Type Two assignments and more Type Three and Type Four assignments. Students asked to peer edit and did so in a disciplined and supportive manner. The teacher gave frequent comparison and contrast and persuasive essays and worked with the students to design seven element assignments with differentiated FCAs. The teacher was able to do more conferencing because the students used independent time well. Students worked hard and completed four Type Five papers per year that were featured during parent's night.

In both of these cases, the teachers used the Collins Writing Program. They emphasized the elements that worked best with the level of maturity of their classes. In both cases, the teachers were caring and respectful of the students, but for the less mature writers, there was more emphasis on the task—more telling and selling. For the more mature writers, there was more participating and delegating.

Good programs, consistently delivered, can help improve students' maturity, and as their maturity progresses, the program adapts. Imagine a class where the students had experience with the Collins Writing Program. They know about the Five Types of Writing Assignments, FCAs, oral reading, and peer editing. They know, because of frequent past practice, how to summarize, compare and contrast, persuade, and incorporate technical vocabulary into their writing. They have experience writing in different roles for different audiences and have the satisfaction of occasionally writing a Type Five piece that represents the sum of their skills. And just imagine you got these kids in September. How far could you go? That's the goal—a structured approach that helps both teachers and students achieve in an atmosphere of respect—all while not killing the teacher with unreasonable correction demands.

COLLINS WRITING PROGRAM
...for all students, subjects, and grades

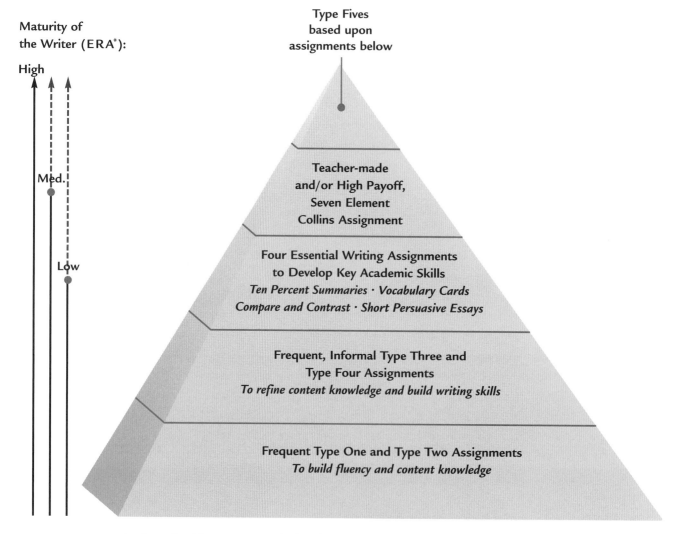

**Maturity of
the Writer (ERA*):**

High

Med.

Low

**Type Fives
based upon
assignments below**

**Teacher-made
and/or High Payoff,
Seven Element
Collins Assignment**

**Four Essential Writing Assignments
to Develop Key Academic Skills**
*Ten Percent Summaries · Vocabulary Cards
Compare and Contrast · Short Persuasive Essays*

**Frequent, Informal Type Three and
Type Four Assignments**
To refine content knowledge and build writing skills

Frequent Type One and Type Two Assignments
To build fluency and content knowledge

As described by Hersey and Blanchard in *Management of Organizational Behavior*, maturity has three components:

1. **Experience with the specific task.** If students have extensive practice writing a summary, they are experienced summary writers.

2. **Willingness to take responsibility.** If students willingly and carefully read the article before summarizing it and review what they have written, they are responsible.

3. **Achievement motivation.** If students are able to write an effective summary but choose not to, they lack motivation to achieve.

The good news is that maturity can be developed in students of all ages through consistent practice, specific feedback, and strong student-teacher relationships. In general, the less mature the writer, the more specific and structured the assignment needs to be. What's your students' ERA*?

*Experience, Responsibility, and Achievement Motivation

CEA **COLLINS EDUCATION ASSOCIATES**
320 Main Street, PO Box 957 • West Newbury, MA 01985 • 1-800-932-4477 • www.collinsed.com

Clarifying Expectations Outside the Classroom

For a writing and thinking program to truly be a program, everyone using it should share common assumptions and expectations. While teachers can be very clear about what they expect, sometimes these expectations become cloudy on the school bus on the way home.

I'd like to share an example that happened years ago but I think we can all relate to it today, whether we view it from a teacher's, student's, parent's, or administrator's perspective. One of my sons, Brendan, was beginning the eighth grade in a new school. I'm not sure about how things work in other families, but September was always a high energy time for us. My wife and I were rested and probably over-involved in our children's school work. As the year went on, and all the other responsibilities crowded in, we became more reasonable. This particular year was no exception.

Brendan had a writing assignment from his social studies teacher over the first weekend of the new school year. It was the fall of 1991, right after Clarence Thomas had been nominated as a Supreme Court Justice. Brendan's assignment, as he told me Friday night, was to write a report on whether Thomas should be confirmed. Remember, this was early September, before Anita Hill's accusations or any of the other controversial information had become known. I responded by saying I thought it was an interesting assignment and asked what he knew about Thomas. Brendan knew almost nothing.

Following my best, highly involved, well-rested-from-homework-supervision-after-summer-vacation instinct, I immediately structured Brendan's Saturday morning for him. "While I'm with Mark at soccer, you get on your bike and go to the library and photocopy at least two magazine articles on Clarence Thomas, come home, read them, and begin writing. Mom will be out, so don't fool around or watch T.V. When I get in at 11:30, I want to see a first draft."

When I got back from soccer, Brendan was shooting baskets in the back yard. "Finished the draft of the Thomas report?" I asked, full of hope.

"No, I went to the library, but it was closed. There was a note that there will be no Saturday hours due to budget cuts."

"What will we do?" I asked.
"We can go to Haverhill; I think they're open."

"Call and check."

We started the half hour drive to Haverhill at 11:45. By 1:30 we had returned home, copies of articles on Clarence Thomas from *Newsweek* and *Time* in hand. Brendan had lunch and began reading. By 2:30 he was writing his first draft, and by 3:00 he was finished. At this point his mother arrived from teaching her Saturday ballet class and reviewed his work. I was cutting the grass—a happy man. When I came in for a break at 3:20, I could tell she was not happy.

"Have you seen Brendan's report on Clarence Thomas?"

"No. What's the problem?"

"I don't think it's very good—just facts about his life. Brendan has no clear opinion and little support. It's more like an encyclopedia article."

"Listen, the guy's been working on the thing almost all day—let it go."

"I don't think that's wise," my wife said. "After all, it's the beginning of the school year and you know the power of first impressions. I think he should make a case for or against his confirmation."

"Let me talk to Brendan. I'll see how he feels."

It was 3:30 and no one was happy.

Brendan, of course, did not know how he felt. He wanted to do a good job, but this report was becoming a major project and if this was the way the new school was going to be, well . . . . We talked for a while and agreed his mother was probably correct. He needed to have a position and support it. While he reread his first draft, I skimmed the articles we had copied and tried to talk to him about possible strengths and weaknesses of Clarence Thomas. By 4:30 he was on a roll. He finished his draft, complete with biographical information and an opinion about the suitability of Thomas' candidacy. He brought it to Mom. She was pleased.

At 5:00 he decided he had put so much into the report he would type it on the computer. It would be perfect. Sometime a little before 5:30, a one-page, double-spaced 250 word report on Clarence Thomas was finished—a triumph for the American family.

The report was turned in on Monday, and I left Tuesday afternoon for three days of workshops. I called in each night to find out how "we" did on the

Clarence Thomas report. On Friday, almost two weeks later, we heard. Brendan got a check. "A check?" I screamed. "All that work and you only got a check?"

"Yes," Brendan said. "My teacher only wanted to make sure we thought about the nomination over the weekend and watched for information on TV and in the paper. He said it was no big deal."

I hope the point of my story is clear. None of us was sure about what was expected. As a result, my wife and I overreacted, turning a Type One assignment into a Type Four. And Brendan, feeding off of our concerns turned it into a Type Five! He wasn't sure what "not a big deal" meant. Is this wrong? Of course not. All three of us learned quite a bit about Clarence Thomas, but Brendan spent a beautiful September Saturday on an assignment that should have taken twenty minutes. However, my real fear is that when a teacher wants a Type Five assignment, some student might interpret it as a Type One and be evaluated negatively because expectations were not stated clearly.

This program is designed to help avoid this problem by clearly communicating to students and their well-meaning parents what is and is not expected. But limiting negative evaluation on four of the five types invariably raises questions about how fellow educators and community members might react. Compositions evaluated positively because the student produced a requisite number of lines (Type One) or because the content was correct (Type Two) or because the work met the requirements set by the focus correction areas (Types Three and Four) leave teachers open to criticism that they have lowered their standards. Yet one of the advantages of using this program is that it provides a common set of definitions and expectations for students, teachers, and the community.

The formatting system for compositions (described in Chapter One), which requires that students label papers Type One or Type Two and list the FCAs, certainly helps communicate the expectations of the program. I've also included on the inside back cover of this book a replication of a poster that briefly defines the five types of writing assignments. It can be a symbol of the program that can help all teachers in a school use the same terminology and help students remember the differences between the five types.

In addition, the letter to parents, on page 112, can be used to briefly summarize the program and encourage questions and comments from them.

Dear Parent(s):

This year your child will be writing a great deal because I want my students to be intellectually active. To achieve this purpose, I will be using the Collins Writing Program, which involves giving five different types of writing assignments. Some assignments are designed simply to help students get their ideas on paper or to discover what they already know about a topic. These assignments are called *Type One* assignments and are evaluated very simply—did the student do it or not? Type One assignments are not designed to be compositions or essays. They are simply ways to guarantee that your son or daughter is thinking about a topic.

Type Two assignments require that students provide the correct information in response to a specific question. In Type Two writing, I do not judge the quality of the writing—just the content. Type One and Type Two writing assignments are designed to be completed quickly and to promote thought.

Type Three and *Type Four* writing assignments are designed to produce ideas and to develop writing skills. Type Three and Type Four writing assignments use a concept called focus correcting. Focus correcting is based on the belief that student writing improves more quickly when the student works to improve a few writing problems at a time. It will be hard for me not to correct every error on every paper, but this year, for Type Three and Type Four assignments, I will be indicating errors on each paper in usually three areas. These areas will be explained and announced in advance so that my students can focus their energies on them. The focus correction areas will be listed on the top left-hand side of each Type Three or Type Four writing assignment.

Type Five writing assignments are the most difficult because they require the student to produce publishable work, that is, work that is as free as possible from all errors. In some cases students will do a Type One assignment, edit and revise it so that it becomes a Type Three or Type Four, and finally polish it so that it becomes a Type Five. The Collins Writing Program will help me encourage my students to think, take chances, formulate ideas, and polish their ideas into finished compositions.

Parents often ask, "How can I help?" Here are a few suggestions: First, be aware of the five types of writing assignments and realize that sometimes writing assignments will not have to be perfect. Be a helper and an encourager, not a critic. Provide a quiet place to write with good lighting and a dictionary. Talk about the assignments and help your daughter or son get many ideas. And, if you are asked to review a composition, read it out loud. Ask if it sounds right. You'll be surprised at how many of their own mistakes they will be able to hear.

If you have any questions or comments about this program or about anything else we are doing, please call.

Sincerely,

Misused/Misspelled Word List I

a lot	height	success
all right	hundred	surprise
allowed	interesting	than
another	it's/its	their/there/they're
are/our	knew	then
asked	laid	they
beautiful	led	threw/through
because	length	to/too/two
believe/belief	lets/let's	tomorrow
bought	library	truly
calendar	lose/loose	Tuesday
children	mother	twelfth
choose/chose	ninety	until
clothes	no/know/now	used to
coming	off	usually
course	once	Wednesday
definite(ly)	passed/past	we're/were
divide	people	weird
doesn't	precede	went
doubt	pretty	where
enough	principle/principal	woman/women
escape	probably	you're/your
every	receive	_____
February	said	_____
finally	school	_____
for/four	science	_____
forty	sense/since	_____
friends	separately	_____
fright	social studies	_____
grammar	some	_____
hear	something	_____
heard	strength	_____

Misused/Misspelled Word List II

absence

accommodate

affect/effect

amateur

apartment

assignment

athletic

attendance

awfully

beginning

business

cafeteria

capital/capitol

commitment

condemn

conscientious

convenient

description

despise

embarrassing

equipment

exaggerate

excellent

existence

fascinate

foreign

generally

government

guarantee

guidance

harass

immediately

independent

indispensable

jealous

knowledge

laboratory

maintenance

mathematics

miniature

misspell

necessary

noticeable

obscene

occasion

occurred

parallel

passed

pastime

permanent

physical

playwright

pleasant

possession

precede

privilege

psychology

publicly

pursue

recommend

repetition

rhythm

ridiculous

schedule

secretary

seize

simile

sincerely

sophomore

specifically

specimen

statue

subtle

technique

tragedy

transferred

tries

tyranny

undoubtedly

whether/weather

_____

_____

_____

_____

_____

_____

_____

_____

_____

_____

_____

Works Cited

Bean, J.C. (2001). *Engaging ideas: The professor's guide to integrating writing, critical thinking, and active learning in the classroom.* San Francisco, CA: Jossey-Bass.

Collins, J.J. (2004). *Selecting and teaching focus correction areas.* West Newbury, MA: Collins Education Associates.

Culham, R. (2003). *6 + 1 Traits of writing: grades 3 and up.* Portland, OR: Northwest Regional Educational Laboratory

Debell, M. (2005, October). *Rates of computer and internet use by children in nursery school and students in kindergarten through twelfth grade.* Issue brief (NCES2005-111rev). Jessup, MD: US Department of Education.

Dempster, F. (1991, April). "Synthesis of research on reviews and tests." *Educational Leadership, 48 (7).*

Elbow, P. (1992, January). *Writing Teacher,* 72.

Frey, N., Fisher, D., & Hernandez, T. (2003, December). "What's the Gist?" Summary Writing for Struggling Adolescent Writers. *Voices from the Middle, 11 (2),* 43–49.

Friedman, T.L. (2005). *The world is flat: A brief history of the twenty-first century.* New York, NY: Farrar, Straus and Giroux.

Glenn, D. (2007, June). "You Will Be Tested On This." *The Chronicle of Higher Education, 53 (40),* A14.

Graham, S., Perin, D. (2007). *Writing next: Effective strategies to improve writing of adolescents in middle and high schools.* Washington, DC: Alliance for Excellent Education.

Hersey, P. & Blanchard, K.H. (1977). *Management of organizational behavior: Utilizing human resources* (Third edition). Englewood Cliffs, NJ: Prentice-Hall Inc.

Hillocks, Jr., G., (2002). *The testing trap: How state writing assessments control learning.* New York, NY: Teachers College Press.

Kasper-Ferguson, S. & Moxley, R.A. (2002, May). "Developing a writing package with student graphing of fluency." *Education and Treatment of Children, 25 (2),* 249–267.

Kilpatrick, J. (1984). *The writer's art.* Fairway, KS: Andrews, McMeel and Parber Inc.

Kissner, E. (2006). *Summarizing, paraphrasing, and retelling: Skills for better reading, writing, and test taking.* Portsmouth, NH: Heinemann.

Marzano, R.J., Pickering, D.J., & Pollock, J.E. (2001). *Classroom instruction that works: Research based strategies for increasing student achievement.* Alexandria, VA: Association for Supervision and Curriculum Development.

Marzano, R.J. (2004). *Building background knowledge for academic achievement.* Alexandria, VA: Association for Supervision and Curriculum Development.

Menand, L. (2004, June). "Bad Comma: Lynne Truss's strange grammar." *The New Yorker.*

Murnane, R.J., Levy, F. (1996). *Teaching the new basic skills: Principles for educating children to thrive in a changing economy.* New York, NY: The Free Press.

Olson, C.B. (1986). *Practical ideas for teaching writing as a process.* Sacramento, CA: California State Department of Education.

Reeves, D.B. (2004). *101 Questions & answers about standards, assessment, and accountability.* Englewood, CO: Advanced Learning Press.

Ruggles Gere, A., Christenbury, L., & Sassi, K. (2005). *Writing on demand: Best practices & strategies for success.* Portsmouth, NH: Heinemann.

Schmoker, M. (2006). *Results now: How we can achieve unprecedented improvements in teaching and learning.* Alexandria, VA: Association for Supervision and Curriculum Development.

Schmoker, M. (2007, April). "Reading, Writing, and Thinking for All." *Educational Leadership, 64 (7),* 63–66.

Schmoker, M. (2003, February). "First Things First: Demystifying Data Analysis." *Educational Leadership, 60 (5).*

Schwab, M. (2007). "Using Artificial Intelligence Software to Provide Feedback for Revision in Writing Instruction." *Diss. Immaculata University*

Spandel, V. (2005). *The nine rights of every writer.* Portsmouth, NH: Heinemann.

Spandel, V., & Stiggins, R.J. (1990). *Creating writers: Linking assessment and writing instruction.* Long Plains, NY: Longman

Truss, L. (2003). *Eats, shoots & leaves, the zero tolerance approach to punctuation.* New York, NY: Penguin Group, Inc.

Wiggins, G., & McTighe, J. (1998). *Understanding by design.* Alexandria, VA: Association for Supervision and Curriculum Development.

Wormeli, R. (2005). *Summarization in any subject.* Alexandria, VA: Association for Supervision and Curriculum Development.

Type

Name

Date

\# _____

FCA   pts.   Name

FCA   pts.   Date

FCA   pts.

Title:

Services from Collins Education Associates

Collins Education Associates (**CEA**) is a consulting and training organization made up of associates selected because of their outstanding teaching ability and commitment to our program. Our most popular workshops and services are described below.

Half-Day and Full-Day Workshops

Developing Writing and Thinking Skills Across the Curriculum: A Practical Program for Schools

This is our basic workshop. It demonstrates ways of using writing activities to increase students' understanding of course content, classroom involvement, and motivation to learn. A key theme is actually saving teacher time and effort in preparing and conducting lessons as well as in processing student work. For teachers of grades 4 and above in all subject areas.

A Writing Program That Works

This workshop demonstrates how to build three critical teaching strategies into an effective program of writing instruction using the Cumulative Writing Folder. For teachers of Language Arts and English (grades 4–12) for whom teaching of writing is a primary responsibility.

Writing in the Elementary Grades

This workshop offers elementary grade teachers practical strategies for helping their students gain writing fluency and comfort with the writing process. The strategies help your students discover writing as a rewarding form of self-expression and a tool for learning in all curriculum areas. For teachers in grades K-6.

Extended Training

CEA also offers three- to seven-day courses. These popular courses reflect the realization that most significant change requires extensive training. The major focus of our courses is on intensive instruction in the use of the Five Types of Writing, Cumulative Writing Folder, and three key teaching strategies: oral reading, focus correcting, and using students' past writing to teach new skills. Other topics include motivating students to write, diagnosing writing weaknesses, using efficient techniques for giving feedback on papers, teaching techniques to improve writing style, writing as a way to foster learning, teaching students how to be resources to themselves during the peer editing process, and creating effective writing assignments.

Because we custom-tailor our training to meet the needs of our clients, we design our multi-day courses only after consulting with the host and the participants. Many of our courses are offered for graduate credit through arrangements with universities throughout the country.

Consulting Services

A basic assumption in our work is that writing instruction is most effective when it is supported by a program—a unified set of teaching techniques and expectations about student writing that is developed and reinforced over a period of years. But program development takes time. Individual teachers can improve the teaching of writing after having attended a half-day or one-day workshop, but it is rare for a school or school system to develop and implement a writing program as a result of a half-day workshop. Based on these realities, we have fashioned a number of program development services that normally only small-group or one-to-one instruction can provide. Listed here are some examples of consultant services available to schools or school systems:

Grade-alike group meeting: Meet with consultant by grade level to discuss implementation issues.

Team meetings: Meet with consultant in teams (different subject areas) to discuss writing and to integrate approaches and strategies.

Demonstrations: Watch consultant teach a writing lesson modeling specific techniques.

Peer coaching: Plan and teach a lesson with consultant.

Selecting FCAs by grade level: Establish a scope and sequence of instruction and align them with learning outcomes.

Troubleshooting and developing common standards: Examine students' writing in order to standardize practice and develop additional strategies for teaching and editing.

Collins Education Associates Publications Order Form

For current prices visit www.collinsed.com

Classroom Management Systems

	QTY.	UNIT PRICE	SUBTOTAL
Cumulative Writing Folder by John Collins, Ed.D. The *Cumulative Writing Folder Program* is a package of 25 easy-to-use folders designed to help manage the classroom writing program in grades four to twelve, with directions. (Set of 25 with *Teacher's Guide*)			
Primary Cumulative Writing Folder by John Collins, Ed.D., and Gary Chadwell A companion to the Cumulative Writing Folder, this primary version (grades one to three) is a package of 25 easy-to-use folders. Each package also contains a set of directions, cards with student writing aids, and a Writers' Marks poster. (Set of 25 with *Teacher's Guide*)			
Teacher's Implementation Folder by John Collins, Ed.D. The Teacher's Implementation Folder provides a convenient management tool to keep track of student writing assignments and notes about the assignment's effectiveness. This folder is a great way to organize student work for team meetings, curriculum discussions and future planning. Teachers typically need one folder for each course taught. (Set of 25 for grades K-12)			

Posters

	QTY.	UNIT PRICE	SUBTOTAL
Five Types of Writing by John Collins, Ed.D. This 22" x 26" poster briefly defines Collins' five different types of writing assignments.			
Writer's Marks by John Collins, Ed.D., and Gary Chadwell This 19" x 24" poster displays six common editing symbols for grades 1 to 3. One poster is included in each package of the Primary Cumulative Writing Folders.			
Revision and Editing Symbols by John Collins, Ed.D. This 22" x 26" poster displays fourteen common editing symbols, with *Teacher's Guide*, for grades 4 to 12.			

Essential Primary Grade FCAs
by John Collins, Ed.D., and Gary Chadwell
This 22" x 26" poster briefly defines Collins' eight Focus Correction Areas for Primary Grades, with *Teacher's Guide*.

Essential Elementary Grade FCAs
by John Collins, Ed.D., and Gary Chadwell
This 22" x 26" poster briefly defines Collins' eight Focus Correction Areas for Elementary Grades, with *Teacher's Guide*.

Essential Middle School FCAs by John Collins, Ed.D.
This 22" x 26" poster briefly defines Collins' six Focus Correction Areas for Middle School, with *Teacher's Guide*.

Essential High School FCAs by John Collins, Ed.D.
This 22" x 26" poster briefly defines Collins' seven Focus Correction Areas for High School, with *Teacher's Guide*.

Books

	QTY.	UNIT PRICE	SUBTOTAL
The Collins Writing Program: Improving Student Performance Through Writing and Thinking Across the Curriculum by John Collins, Ed.D.			
Implementing the Cumulative Writing Folder Program: A Comprehensive Guide with Answers to the Most Frequently Asked Questions by John Collins, Ed.D.			
Developing an Effective Writing Program for the Elementary Grades by Gary Chadwell			
Selecting and Teaching Focus Correction Areas: A Planning Guide by John Collins, Ed.D.			
Writing Projects for the Elementary Grades: Prompts, Ideas, and Assignments for Grades 3-6 by Gary Chadwell			
Writing Strategies for the Primary Grades: Prompts and Ideas for Grades K-3 by Gary Chadwell			
High School Writing Projects: Prompts and Projects for Thinking and Learning Across the Curriculum by John Collins, Ed.D., and Gary Chadwell			
Middle School Writing Projects: Ideas for Writing Across the Curriculum by Gary Chadwell			
A Survivor's Guide to the Research Paper: Five Structured Assignments to Lead Students Through Their First Research Paper by John Collins, Ed.D.			
Summarizing, Persuading, and Preparing for the SAT: A Writing Project for College-Bound, High School Students by John Collins, Ed.D.			
Writing About Literature: Ideas for the High School English Teacher by Mark Dressel			
Letters from a Trunk: A Writing Project About Twentieth-Century America by Callie Kingsbury and Carol Gentry			
Improving Writing Skills in Career and Technology High Schools by John Collins, Ed.D. and Suzanne Doherty, Ed.D.			

Classroom Materials

	QTY.	UNIT PRICE	SUBTOTAL
Editing Phone Plastic "phone" that motivates students to read out loud during the revision and editing process. All grades.			

For current prices visit www.collinsed.com
Shipping will be added to all orders.

Please make check/purchase order payable to:
Collins Education Associates LLC
320 Main Street
PO Box 957
West Newbury, MA 01985
800-932-4477 • Fax 978-363-2212

Subtotal	
Shipping	
Total enclosed	

Ship to

Name _____

Address _____

City _____ State _____ Zip _____